# Nick Wood

Nick was an actor, a freelance journalist, and a teacher before he became a full-time writer. His commissions include BBC Radio 4, Derby Theatre, Thalia Theatre Hamburg, Action Transport, Theatr Iolo, Hans Otto Potsdam, Eastern Angles, and Nottingham Playhouse.

He has worked with the RSC as a Learning Associate running workshops for teachers and young people, was the writer on the community projects for five regional tours, and part of the team for a learning residency in North Carolina.

His plays have had over fifty productions in Europe and the USA and Canada. With Andrew Breakwell he started New Theatre Nottingham and recently returned to acting and toured *A Girl With A Book*.

He lives in Nottingham, UK.

First published in the UK in 2016 by Aurora Metro Publications Ltd
67 Grove Avenue, Twickenham, TW1 4HX
www.aurorametro.com    info@aurorametro.com

Production: Simon Smith
With thanks to: Neil Gregory, Tracey Mulford and Lucia Tunstall.

Printed in the UK by 4edge Limited.
ISBN: 978-1-910798-61-4 (print)
ISBN: 978-1-910798-62-1 (ebook)

# A Girl With A Book
## and other plays

## Nick Wood

AURORA METRO BOOKS

# CONTENTS

# INTRODUCTION

When I was appointed to the post of Artistic Director at Nottingham Playhouse I knew that I wanted to return new writing to the heart of its artistic policy. When I first moved to the East Midlands in 1999 it didn't take long for me to be introduced to a very active group of writers with a definite idea about how I should go about it; put regional playwrights first.

With more than 50 new plays produced since then the wisdom of that decision has been confirmed over and over again and Nottinghamshire voices have been instrumental in the shaping of our repertoire. The success of the policy has contributed in its turn to the decision that Nottingham should be awarded UNESCO City of Literature status.

There was one Nottingham writer whose work was already being championed at the Playhouse by the then Head of Education, Andrew Breakwell, and that writer was Nick Wood. His play *Warrior Square* had been commissioned and was scheduled for a small-scale tour in 2001, a decision which allowed Nick to stop teaching and commit full-time to being a writer. It's the story of two young people who have arrived in the UK as immigrants having fled their country and are having to come to terms with their painful history and their new surroundings. As with so many of Nick's plays it was a simply told story that in production proved to be so much more than it appeared to be on the page. The fact that there has barely been a time since then that it's been out of production in Europe is a testament to Nick's qualities as a writer as well as giving the lie to the idea that regional voices are necessarily parochial.

Since 2001, the Playhouse has produced six more of his plays: *Bloody Brecht*; *Birdboy* (co-produced with Action Transport); *Can You Whistle, Johanna?* (Adapted from the play by Ulf Stark); *Children Of The Crown*; *Mia* (co-produced with the Thalia Theatre in Hamburg) and *My Name Is Stephen Luckwell*. We have also supported the development of *A Girl With A Book* and we're co-producing with ajtc Theatre Company his adaptation of Mick Jackson's novel *The Underground Man* in 2017.

It's worth pointing out that this is only a small part of his output over the same period and he's had plays premiered by companies as wide-ranging as Eastern Angles, Theatr Iolo in Cardiff, the Crucible in Sheffield and Kazaliste Voriovitica in Croatia amongst many others, which means that he is one of the UK's most produced playwrights. The fact that most of them have been produced regionally (or in Europe) means they have rarely received national reviews, but despite that, his work will have been seen by more people than the plays of many of his better known contemporaries.

Of the four that are in this volume two were premiered at Nottingham Playhouse, another was presented by us in an early workshop version and the final one, *A Dream of White Horses,* hasn't had a production in the UK at the time of publication.

## The Plays

*A Girl With A Book* is inspired by the story of Malala Yousafzai but rather than simply retell the events of her life, Nick puts himself at the centre of the play in order to explore whether a "middle-aged, middle-class white man" could ever understand the world of a young Pakistani girl. It is the odd one out in this collection as it is written about a young person – Malala, but it is designed to be performed to both young and adult audiences and in this case the setting is the theatre itself with all the power and complexity that brings.

I should own up to my scepticism when Nick first came to talk to me about the play as I couldn't see how it could work and was worried that it would seem self-indulgent, not least because Nick was going to perform it himself. I agreed to support the development but not to commission it. Nick went ahead and we presented an early version of it for one night in the Neville Studio; I was proved totally wrong. It's intelligent, insightful and moving and Nick is speaking for many of us when he voices his internal conflicts, his embarrassment and his anger. With this play he has allowed a conversation to happen with others that many of us can only have with ourselves.

Nick developed the play further and then toured it to great acclaim in the UK. As with so much of his work it has gone on to be performed internationally where the character of the author becomes an everyman. In Germany alone the play has already had eight productions and I have no doubt that that number will increase.

*A Dream of White Horses* tells the story of Paul whose father fell to his death while soloing A Dream of White Horses, a sea cliff climb in Wales. Paul wants to attempt the Dream and to try and find out whether his father's death was an accident or suicide.

I turned the play down for the Playhouse (as did other theatres in England) and subsequently it had its premiere in Germany where it's since been produced three times. Once again the setting is of supreme importance and it allows for some thrilling staging opportunities with much of the play taking place whilst the characters are climbing. Interestingly, it is those very staging opportunities that have made the production of it so long delayed here. Hopefully, one of you reading this will see the challenge as an opportunity and make this sentence redundant.

*Birdboy* was another co-production and like most of Nick's plays it toured widely. It's partly set on a knoll that's the site of King Caradoc's last battle against the Romans and it explores the unlikely friendship between Eddie and Tim, one a bully and the other a loner. As they find themselves isolated both at home and in the village, they create a den at the knoll where they can feel safe and be themselves.

The play explores the themes of bullying, trust and friendship in a way that is both playful and moving with the final sequence powerfully drawing the strands together whilst leaving the sort of ambiguity that one could wish to see in more plays for adults. Also on rereading I was struck that in this post-*Game of Thrones* world that the boys imagined world of sword fights in an isolated snowy setting feels even more plausible now than it did in 2005.

*Mia* is both set in a classroom and designed to be performed in a classroom and the trick (and it's a magical one) is that the students who are attending the lesson should have no idea of what's going to take place. At the beginning of the lesson a young refugee arrives and she tells the students that she's of Roma background and that she has received a postcard from her lost sister that has been posted from the local area. She then shows them a photograph and asks if anyone in the class has seen her sister and it's there that the conversation begins.

The production of *Mia* had far more impact than any of us could have foreseen. It was co-commissioned and produced with the Thalia Theatre in Hamburg and was given simultaneous productions in both countries. As both theatres were at that time members of the European Theatre Convention it was seen by directors and dramaturgs from theatre companies across the continent. This led to the commissioning of classroom plays from twelve writers which were then produced on exactly the same model as *Mia* by twenty-four European theatres. There can't be many other playwrights who can say that their work has initiated a new movement.

I'm sure that you will have worked out by now that the settings for all these plays have a poetic and mythic resonance, whilst the subjects and the concerns are universal and that combination is one of the reasons why they translate so well to other cultures; it's also why they don't seem to date and therefore warrant publication.

I have got to know Nick well over the years and his lively imagination combined with his enthusiasm for the development of new talent has meant that he is always open to new ideas and new opportunities. He is clearly driven to explore the experiences of those whom he regards as being on the fringes of society or are striving to improve the lives of others, but he's anything but a dull cove or a drearily pious person. His interest is in telling good and meaningful stories in as theatrically engaging a manner as possible and it's no surprise that his three favourite writers are Brecht, Beckett and Shakespeare.

All the plays in this collection are written with young people in mind, though they're not all plays written for young audiences. They are passionate, engaging, questioning and challenging and, like *Warrior Square*, I have no doubt they will continue to be performed in the UK and around the world for many years to come.

*Giles Croft, Artistic Director, Nottingham Playhouse*

# A GIRL WITH A BOOK

First performed at The Neville Studio, Nottingham Playhouse, UK, 10th June 2013.

Directed by Andrew Breakwell.

## Cast

The Writer                    Nick Wood

*The play is set in the room where the writer works. The writer can be played by an actor of any age, ethnicity or gender.*

*A chair with a desk and a laptop on it. Another chair downstage. A small rug in front of the desk. Books, pamphlets, notebooks, folders, newspaper cuttings are on the desk, on the floor. Behind the desk is a third chair with a cardboard box on it. The writer comes in with a cup of coffee. Sits. Checks his notebook. Checks through the print out of Malala's blog. Stretches and begins to tap the keys. He's concentrating but it doesn't seem as though he's writing.*

**WRITER** Bugger!

I don't care what anyone says – I am working. This is work. You ask any writer. You can't expect the words to come pouring out all day long. It doesn't happen like that – you can get stuck. Then if you do something else, something mindless, like playing Spider Solitaire, if you're lucky, suddenly out of nowhere an idea can pop into your head and the problem's solved itself. Not everyone understands that. My wife'll come up here – and say –

'Couldn't the something mindless be something that's useful at the same time?'

Like what?

'Putting the hoover round the house? Mowing the lawn? Sorting out the tap in the bathroom you were going to fix months ago?'

You're missing the point. You have to concentrate to... hoover. What Spider Solitaire allows me to do is let my mind go completely blank...

It's a bit like meditation really. No, it's not. It's time wasting.

I can tell you when exactly. Half past four. 9th October. Last year. I'd been writing all day. Pages and pages. None of them any good. Decided that was it and deleted the lot.

*He clicks onto the BBC website and reads.*

Malala Yousafzai: Pakistan activist, 14, shot in Swat.

Gunmen have wounded Malala Yousafzai, a 14-year-old rights activist who has campaigned for girls' education in the Swat Valley in north-west Pakistan.

A fourteen year old girl shot for wanting to go to school?

Two other girls were shot. Kainat Riaz and Shazia Ramzan, got hit as well. Malala in the head. Kainat in the shoulder. Shazia below her left collarbone and in her left hand as she tried to protect herself. Four bullets. Fired point blank into the back of a school bus by a man in a balaclava. Why would anyone do a thing like that? There's a statement out already. From the TTP, who are...? The Pakistani Taliban.

The TTP successfully targeted Malala Yousafzai. Although she was young and a girl and the TTP does not believe in attacking women, whoever leads a campaign against Islam and Sharia is ordered to be killed by Sharia. If anyone thinks that Malala is targeted because of education, that's absolutely wrong, and propaganda from the media.

Madness.

For crying out loud, she's only fourteen. And they think they can justify what they've done in the name of religion? Well, they're not the first ones to try that one. Make your own list. Fourteen.

Who is she? How did this happen?

*He gets up from the desk.*

I knew that night I wanted to write... something. When you first get an idea your mind starts racing with all the possibilities. It should be simple. I've got the story. The trick'll be to find the right way in. And then, a few days later Ban Ki Moon came out with this – 'The terrorists showed what frightens them most: a girl with a book.' He's given me the title. All I've got to do is... write it.

I made notes, I made coffee. I went on Google, I walked the dog. I read books about Pakistan and Islam. I might even have played the odd game of Spider Solitaire. But *A Girl With A Book*, cast of four, three female, one male. Male actor to double Malala's father and the gunman – it's not going to work, doesn't feel right.

I played around with it off and on for a week before I ground to a halt with a blank page and a question. What have I, a white, middle aged, middle class playwright of no fixed belief, living safely in the west, got to say on a subject about which I know nothing at all?

You can't do everything via Google. No, you can't. Really. I'm going to have to go out. Talk to people. Ask questions. Approach the whole thing with an open mind. Except... I have this sneaking suspicion the last thing I've got is an open mind.

I start with the Islamic information stall outside Marks & Spencers – May I ask a question?

– Do you know, sir, the first question we always get asked about Islam? Why do we men make Muslim women dress like they do?

I wasn't going to ask that actually, but now you mention it, I don't really get it either.

– When you see a woman, sir, in the street, and she is all exposed, you look at her. You can't help yourself. I'm a married man, but I look too. If that woman is covered, then we don't see her only as an object of sexual desire.

I don't think women should be treated only as objects of sexual desire, but if they are, it's not the woman's fault, is it, it's the man's? Look, I was in Washington in the summer, it was blazing hot...

– I know what you are going to say, sir.

There's this Muslim family, the husband, children, all wearing light summer clothes. Except the wife. She's in black from head to foot, even her eyes are behind a gauze screen. She must have been dying in there.

– But that woman understands her discomfort is nothing compared to the heat she would have to endure if she went straight into the fires of hell.

What can you say? I don't argue. I can't. We chat some more. At least we can agree the way Muslims are suddenly to blame for everything is wrong and bad for us all. I want to try to understand but we're miles apart. We smile, shake hands, and I thank him as I walk away with a copy of the Koran and an armful of books on Islam.

The fires of hell for dressing in appropriate summer clothing?

And he got me too. 'Do you know the first question we always get asked about Islam?' That wasn't going to be my first question.

I mean everyone's free to dress how they like but there's no sense to it. Even if you say it's your choice you're covering up why wouldn't you want to feel the rain on your face and the wind in your hair? And it is always men telling women what to do.

But what does make sense? Tattoos? Top hats? Getting your nose pierced? Bishops and cardinals in frocks? I've got no objection to nuns and they cover their heads.

There's lots of stuff I don't get about organised religion. For one, they're all so keen on sin and punishment. They talk about compassion. Mercy. Forgiveness. But you don't seem to see very much of it, do you? Catholics and Protestants have been killing each other for centuries. They're all at it. In Burma we've got Buddhists killing Muslims – Buddhists for God's sake? And...

This is not getting anything written.

*He goes back to the desk.*

But what if you do feel you are the ones always getting blamed for everything? What if you and your family live with the daily threat of being killed by bombs dropped from unmanned drones?

Can't be much fun over here. You wear the hijab. You've got a beard. I bet you can feel people looking at you everywhere you go.

*He gets up. He can't settle to work.*

It's so tangled. I can't make sense of what I feel about any of it. Don't get me wrong, I'm not prejudiced. I can't be, can I? I read the Guardian.

You know those sentences that start I'm not racist / sexist / homophobic / whatever else the speaker wants you to believe they aren't and then they stick in the word but and go on to prove that's exactly what they are?

Yeah, well, my sentence would have to be – I'm all for diversity but wouldn't the world be a much simpler and safer place if everybody thought like me?

Then I get it. Of course I've got to do the research, but I don't have to beat myself up because I don't know everything there is to know about Islam and Pakistan. I can still tell the story. What it's about is what it's always been about – ordinary people doing extraordinary things. I'll still go out and talk to those who know more about it than I do. Maybe I can get some of them to let me try bits out on them. But I'll put away the books until I need them. Get rid of Google, and go back to the beginning. 2009. The eleven year old Malala, at home with her family in Mingora, a small town in the Swat Valley.

It's night time. Evening prayers are over. Malala's playing games on the computer with her brother. She looks at her Harry Potter rucksack and her blue uniform hanging from a hook on the back of the door. She thinks about what she's going to wear to school.

– I can't wear my school uniform, I can't wear my pink dress because the Taliban will think it's too colourful.

Her father Ziauddin listens. He's the principal of the girls' school so he's her head teacher as well as her dad. He takes a piece of paper out of his pocket. It's a print out of a blog from the BBC Urdu website written by a girl called Gul Makai. He reads it to them –

'My mother made me breakfast and I went off to school. I was afraid going to school because the Taliban had issued an edict banning all girls from attending schools. Only 11 students attended the class out of 27. Perhaps there will be more tomorrow.'

'A friend of mine gave me this today. He told me to read it. I wanted to say Gul Makai is really my daughter. Your mother thinks we should change your name to Gul Makai. She thinks it's a much nicer name than Malala.'

'Malala was a warrior, I'd rather be named after a hero, than a cornflower,' says her brother.

'That's because you're a boy and all you can think about is fighting,' says his sister.

'Shall I read some more?' asks her father.

'Time for bed,' says her mother.

She bustles the children away, leaving the last paragraph of the blog unread...

*He returns to the desk and finds the print out of the blog and reads it out.*

> 'On my way from school to home I heard a man saying 'I will kill you'. I hastened my pace and after a while I looked back if the man was still coming behind me. But to my utter relief he was talking on his mobile and must have been threatening someone else over the phone.'

> Eleven years old when she wrote that. Another girl was supposed to do it but she changed her mind, and Ziauddin put forward his daughter to take her place.

> Could I have asked my daughter to write that blog?

*He finds another passage in the printed blog.*

> I have a heavy bag, I go to school, I come home, I do my homework...

*He steps away from the desk remembering Ziauddin's words.*

> My daughter complained about school, but when it was banned she knew how much she wanted it.

> People said to me: How can you let her do this? We had to stand up. She knew what would come. We saw many atrocities, many cruelties. When the elders are silent, the children have to speak up.

When the elders are silent, the children have to speak up...

I take the couple of pages I've written so far into a year ten English class at a girls' school to see what they think. And to ask that question: If I were Ziauddin, what would I have done?

A face in the front row looks up at me from under her hijab and listens as the other girls put forward their opinions.

– You'd have to live there to know...

– It's a different way of life...

– Different culture...

– Perhaps she wanted to do it...

Then she puts up her hand to speak. Brought up in Libya. She knows more than I'll ever know about living with danger. 'When you know that everywhere you go, I'm not sure how to say this, death is walking very near to you, you are afraid, but you think differently about life, about being alive. It's important, but not so important.'

A few weeks later I'm trying out a new section with a group of community workers when, after the first few pages, a striking black woman takes out a notepad and starts writing. Right in front of me. I try to ignore her and concentrate on the others but my eyes keep being drawn back. What's she writing? A shopping list? I'm willing her – put down the pen and listen to me.
When I've finished she's the first one to speak. 'What that girl said, about death walking near you, I know that pain. It made me remember. I wrote something. Sorry. But I had to.' She and her family were badly beaten up by the National Front in the 80s. She reads me what she was writing –

'You have to stand up. Why hide? Hiding is more painful. Like being in darkness. When you stop hiding it's freedom. You stand up and walk in the light. What price is freedom? How much is the cost for freedom? Maybe a life?'

When will I stop jumping to conclusions about people? The last time I stood up for anything I was ten years old and Martin Mayfield had tried to pinch my bike.

Where does anyone find that kind of courage?

I go back on line and start watching the interviews. In one she's sitting next to her father, talking about what she wants to be when she grows up when he interrupts her.

– I want to be a doctor that is my dream.

– I think she could do so much more. She should become a politician. People would listen to her. She should work to build a society where any girl can become a medical student and finish her studies.

Her face says, that's his dream, not mine. Ziauddin talks about why he won't leave Swat, the debt he owes to the valley and its people, and how if he has to die honouring that debt then he can't think of a better way. He asks her – What do you think about those nights when I don't sleep here? In the house? In case they come looking for me?

She makes this little noise and hides her head in her hands. She's frightened. Then she looks up, straight at the camera. Nobody's going to make that girl do something she doesn't want to, not even her dad.

What's it like in Swat? I've got no mental picture.

*He types.*

Images of the Swat valley. It's beautiful. I didn't expect this – all these adverts. Luxury hotels, holiday homes, adventure holidays, skiing, white water rafting. It's got the lot. Until 2009, when the Taliban arrive.

There are still rows of tables with starched white napkins in the Continental Hotel but no guests. There are colourful piles of silk in the China Market, but no customers. A banner hangs over the entrance – 'Women are requested to avoid shopping in China Market.'

Public floggings are announced. Attendance expected. There are executions at the crossroads. One night, on the radio, they hear this.

*He plays the Taliban warning of the closure of girls' schools on his iPhone.*

After January 15th girls must not go to school otherwise the guardians and the schools will be held responsible.

50,000 girls will be staying at home. To go, almost overnight from being the ideal tourist destination to that...

Why so frightened about educating women? Nobody's throwing acid at women who want to go to university but I don't think we've got a particularly brilliant record over here.

*He goes on line. Types.*

Women's education. 1897 riots in Cambridge. When it looked like women might be allowed to become full members of the university men marched through the streets pelting women suspected of being students with rotten fruit, some were stoned.

1921 – more riots – when women are awarded degrees the same as the men.

*Types.*

Women's rights. UK. Timeline.

It took the suffragettes till 1918 to get the vote. Then another ten years before women could vote at the same age as men. Up to 1944 a woman had to leave teaching if she got married. Until 1975 you could sack a woman for being pregnant. And so it goes on. Yeah, and that's right, I was talking to somebody the other week who said Boots got it in the neck for putting toys from the Science Museum in the boys section but not in the girls. And this is 2013.

Why did the Taliban move into Swat?

*Goes to his notes.*

Close to the safety of the mountains and the border. Good base for attacks on Islamabad. Classic guerilla tactics. But the rich and powerful had their holiday villas in Swat so it was never going to be long before the army was called in.

The schools are closed. The fighting's getting closer. What was she thinking?

*He finds the blog and reads it.*

I wake up to the roar of heavy artillery fire early in the morning. I'm bored with sitting at home. Some of my friends have already left Swat. It's very dangerous. I can't leave home. I can't go out. I wish my father would take us away from here.

*He starts to imagine the scene. He sits and begins to type as he speaks.*

– Tomorrow we're leaving.

– Where are we going?

– To Islamabad.

*He stops typing but stays at the desk, imagining the voices in the scene.*

– The one good thing about the war is that our father has taken us to many other cities. Islamabad, Peshawar, Bannu. And now we are staying with my aunt. It's good to sit in her garden, watching my brothers play, feeling the silence and the peace. My father comes into the garden. He wants my little brother.

– Malala, where's your brother?

– Playing.

– What's he doing?

– I don't know.

– He's digging a hole. Why is he digging a hole?

– Ask him.

– Hey? What are you doing? What's the game? Why are you digging a hole in uncle's lawn?

– I'm making a grave.

What's that little boy seen to make him want to play at grave digging?

Three weeks later they're back home in Mingora. Someone's broken into their house but the only thing missing is the TV. Her uniform and school bag are hanging where she left them and to her brother's disgust their school opens tomorrow. A truce is called. The fighting stops. Peace talks start. People come back onto the streets. Shops open. Women return to the China Market. But if the extremists have disappeared they haven't gone far. A journalist who took a stand against them is killed, their threats are still on the radio. And the identity of the school girl who wrote a blog for the BBC is no longer a secret.

How could it be kept a secret? She put in too much personal detail. Where she went with her parents. Her friends at school getting bored with hearing about her trip to Bunbair. Didn't anyone at the BBC say, hang on, if you put that bit in everyone will know it's you? Perhaps they did. Perhaps she didn't want them to change a word.

*He goes to his notebook and reads.*

Nowhere does it say that girls should not be allowed to go to school. I have my right to play, to sing, to talk, to go to the market, to stand up. I will have my dream. I will have my education.'

She's on TV, she's on chat shows, she's interviewed on news programmes, she's awarded the Pakistan Youth Prize. She's famous. Come on, it must have been exciting.

Watch the videos and you're watching a child grow up. Far too soon. Far too fast.

*He checks in his notebook.*

The Taliban are back. And this time the army are in earnest. Warnings go out, giving the day and the time the bombardment will start. The rich leave first, followed by thousands of refugees desperate to get away from the fighting. The Yousafzai family go with them. They'll be away for three months.

The children and their mother go to relatives. Ziauddin goes to Peshawar with other senior figures from Swat to lobby the government. He shares a room with two other men. One room where they eat, sleep, pray, and plan their strategy. Every day they are out meeting politicians, addressing crowds in the street, organising press conferences, orchestrating the protests.

'A mother doesn't give milk to a baby that doesn't cry – you have to scream for everything! '

The Taliban announce Ziauddin is now a target. It doesn't stop him, he and his friends keep up the pressure, but they're feeling the strain of being away from their wives and children.

– We get bored with each other.

– The three of us in the same room.

– Always talking about the same things.

Then Ziauddin does something no father should ever do.

– He has forgotten my birthday. I told him yesterday it was my birthday tomorrow. I have a birthday cake for me. My birthday has been celebrated. He's not here. I am happy for the people who made me the cake, but I am not happy for him.

– She has sent me a text in English. She is not happy with me. She wants ice cream, I shall see her soon and I shall take her for ice cream. There's so much to do. The campaign to free Swat. I am optimistic. I am very optimistic. I believe that things will change. I believe that the Taliban will go from Swat. They will be defeated.

Malala has a new ambition. 'I have changed my dream from being a doctor to being a politician because I want to help my people' She shares her father's dreams but she sees him more clearly now. Even though the army says they've defeated the Taliban she has her doubts. 'He is too optimistic. I have a fear in my heart that the Taliban can re-collect their power.'

Father and daughter meet again on the road home. And I find this amazing. Considering the danger they're in. They stop. Ziauddin and the other leaders have a meeting with Richard Holbrook. The American ambassador. He brings Malala with him. She takes part. She asks for help 'I request you all, and I request you, Mr Ambassador, if you will help us with our education.' It's not a secret meeting either. It's filmed by the cameras that have been following them around for months. That's how we know that afterwards Malala goes shopping for DVDs and, at last, she gets her ice cream.

Mingora's deserted, the school's been used as a military base, there are shell holes in the walls, but their house is still standing and her school books are still there. Almost as soon as they get back, the film is put on the internet. By

The New York Times. How did they think that was going to go down? Cooperating with America. If you're living next to a wasps' nest what's the first thing you do? Go up and poke it with a stick?

She's only twelve years old and she's become a political activist. Oh, and then did the hate came pouring out.

'She is a symbol of the infidels and obscenity.'

You see this girl. Writing for the BBC. Being filmed by an American journalist for an American newspaper. Being praised by the American president.

*He gets up.*

If I was living on the border of Pakistan? Would my anger against those who're dropping the bombs turn itself on Malala because I saw her as being on their side? Possibly. Would I think she was being used? Probably. Would I consider killing her to be a righteous act? No. And when the TTP tried neither did the millions who poured onto the streets in protest.

If unmanned drones were flying over my home Thackeray's Lane, and my family was in danger of being killed by a misdirected bomb you'd find it hard to win over my heart and mind.

He looks for a printout of Malala's statements and reads them, remembering the things Ziauddin said as he does so.

– I think of what might happen often and imagine the scene clearly. Even if they come to kill me, I will tell them what they are trying to do is wrong, that education is our basic right.

Nothing's going to shut them up. Her or her dad.

– Girls' education is not considered as important as boys' education.

– Girls will be able to go to school. I will have my education.

– The reality is that girl's education is not only under threat from terrorism.

– I think if the President's daughters went to school in Swat the schools would not have been closed.

– You must give a daughter all her basic rights.

– I will have my dream.

The bell rings for the end of the school day. It's a Tuesday. Tuesdays are safe. You feel nervous on a Friday, not a Tuesday, because Friday is the day of prayer and some believe if you sacrifice yourself on a Friday when you arrive in paradise you will be all the more blessed.

Fourteen girls and three teachers climb into the school bus, an open truck, a canvas cover over the bench seats keeps off the sun and a blue curtain flapping at the back keeps out some of the dust.

They have prepared for this day. The route has been studied. They know when the bus will leave. Where it will stop. How long it will take on each stage of its journey. They have chosen their spot carefully. A car waits to take them into the mountains and across the border.

The bus comes slowly round a sharp bend. The next stop will be Malala's. Less than two hundred metres past the military checkpoint, within plain sight of the soldiers, the bus comes to a halt. The girls can't see the gunmen who've fired the warning shots that made the driver stop and they mistake those shots for the sound of the engine misfiring.

The curtain is pulled back and a man in a black balaclava asks

– Where is Malala? Who is Malala?

– We thought it was a joke, a story from a dream.

– They will have recognised her, anyone can recognise her, we used to cover our faces but she never covered hers.

– The moment she said 'I am Malala' he opened fire, and she was down.

Four bullets. Three girls. Kainat, Malala, Shazia. He missed his target three times. He was only a few feet away from her. What was he thinking as he pointed his gun at a bus load of children? Did his hand shake?

The gunmen escape and the girls are rushed to the nearest hospital. Malala, the most seriously hurt, goes straight into intensive care. They stabilise her and as soon as it's safe to, she's airlifted, Ziauddin at her side, to a military hospital in Peshawar for emergency surgery.

*He sits in the chair stage left. Looks up as if he was looking at the gunman. Flinches and ducks down.*

She must have been leaning forward. Ducking for cover.

*He goes to the chair behind the desk and takes a polystyrene head wrapped in a scarf out of the cardboard box, puts it on the desk and unwraps it. He pushes a pencil into the hole he's made to illustrate the path of the bullet, turns, and holds it up.*

The bullet came downwards, missing her brain, shattering her ear, grazing her jaw, and taking away a piece of her skull. The surgeons clean up the wound and tuck the piece of bone inside her abdomen, keeping it safe, alive, in case it was decided to graft it back onto her head. Isn't that clever?

She can move her arms and legs but no-one can say if she'll live. They've done what they can, but she needs specialist facilities, expert treatment. Sedated and on a ventilator she's flown to Rawalpindi...

*He wraps the head in the scarf and puts it back in the box.*

...and then, finally, to the Queen Elizabeth Hospital in Birmingham where they've become world experts on treating the kind of wounds Malala has suffered. They've had to – it's where they send the most seriously injured British service men and women.

Her family are with her in the hospital. The news of her progress is good. She can talk, she is able to hear with her one good ear. She can take a few steps. Her brain is still exposed, so the biggest danger will be from infection. They send her home, to rest, to get strong enough for the next step.

Some weeks later she's back in hospital ready for the operation that will rebuild her shattered ear and repair the hole in her skull. The bone they planted in her abdomen has shrunk, and may shrink further. To graft it on now would mean more operations in the future.

*He picks up a saucer, tips the paper clips onto the desk and uses it to illustrate what they intend to do with the plate.*

Instead the technicians make a titanium plate for the surgeons to fit over the hole in her skull. Both operations are successful. After months of living with a hole in her head, her exposed brain has been covered. She will be well again.

*He puts the paper clips back in the saucer and goes behind the desk.*

Malala and her family aren't the only heroes. While she was in hospital in Birmingham the thirteen other girls who were on the bus went back to school.

*He picks up and reads the statements from the three girls.*

'I love to study, and nothing will stop me,' said Kainat, 'not even a bullet.'

'Even if they attack me three more times,' said Shazia, I will always go back to school.'

The suspected gunman, a chemistry graduate from Swat, escaped over the border to Afghanistan. His sister, Rehanna Haleem, who still lives in Swat spoke about her brother.

– He has brought shame on our family, what he did was intolerable. I don't consider him my brother anymore.

That's courage.

*He gets up from behind the desk.*

I'm getting closer to writing this thing I know it. I could start writing it now but for all this other stuff going round in my head. The questions. The TTP have one – I know, they're the ones who tried to kill her, but it doesn't stop it being a good question. If we care so much about Malala and her friends why don't we make as much noise about all those the children who are dying whose names we don't know? Especially as some of them are probably being killed by drones controlled by someone in an office on an airfield in Lincolnshire.

This event is different. And to acknowledge that difference doesn't diminish the suffering that others experience. Kainat, Shazia, and Malala weren't innocent victims caught in a bombing raid, or wounded by shell fire not meant for them. They were targeted because a child stood up and said – this is wrong and she made people listen. You can call it defending your religion, you can call it a war, you can call it a jihad, you can call it what you like. But you don't shoot three girls for wanting to go to school.

*The writer sees the note he's made about Ziauddin. He reads it.*

'I'm optimistic about the behaviour of men towards their daughters. We have so many fathers, so many brothers who want education for their sisters and their daughters.'

*He picks up the statement from Malala and reads it.*

Why shouldn't girls go to school? I want my education. I want to go to university. Education is a right for me. It is a right for all the girls in Swat, in Pakistan, in the world.

Fingers crossed.

*He stretches and starts to write.*
*He stops and stares straight ahead.*

*Lights down.*

*The end.*

# A DREAM OF WHITE HORSES

First produced at Theater Ingolstadt in Germany, 25th November 2004.

Directed by Pierre Politz.

## Cast

| | |
|---|---|
| Paul | Enrico Spohn |
| Stevie | Rebecca Kirchmann |
| Martin | Alexander Leistritz |
| Rick | Gregor Trakis |

## Characters

Paul Saunders – wants to be a climber like his father. 16 years old.

Stevie Pitts – she's known Paul since they were both small. 16.

Martin McCormack – has just moved down from Scotland. 16.

Rick Saunders – Paul's father. He was killed on A Dream of White Horses two years previously.

A Dream of White Horses is a climb on Gogarth on Anglesey. It was first led by Ed Drummond in 1968 and is regarded as a classic route. The description of the climb at the start of the play is based on the description in *Rock Climbing in Wales* by Ron James (Constable 1969).

## A brief climbing glossary

Abb – Abseil.

Descender – a device used to control the speed of descent when abseiling down a climb.

Krab – carabiner – a clip essential to all aspects of climbing and rope work.

Friends, nuts – these are used to fit into cracks on the climb so that the rope can be threaded through. This stops the climber falling beyond the point where the Friend / nut has been placed.

Pendule – a controlled swing across the rock face to reach a hold.

Screwgate – a carabiner with a sleeve that screws over the opening to lock it.

Stitch plate – a small metal plate that stops the rope slipping when you're belaying the climber above.

*The music should be chosen to suit the time and setting of the production. 'Mr Tambourine Man' is essential because it is Rick's music.*

## 1. On top of a building

*Darkness.*

*Sounds of climbing.*

*Paul's voice is heard.*

**PAUL**      Step and reach. Step and reach. Keep the momentum going. Concentrate. Concentrate. Feet on the ledges, hands on the pipes. All the holds are there, all the way up. Fingers starting to slip. Not bad enough to stop. Keep going. Keep going. Keep going... YES!

*Music very loud. Spot on Paul hanging from the top of a building by both hands, he takes a spray can from his harness and tags the top.*

*He pulls himself up and over and disappears only to reappear below like lightning.*

## 2. Paul's room.

*Darkness. Music stops as the light hits Paul kneeling in front of a CD player. He puts in a CD and skips through the track – Mr Tambourine Man – until he gets to verse four:*

*'Yes, to dance beneath the diamond sky with one hand waving free*

*Silhouetted by the sea...'*

*He skips back to 'Yes, to dance...' starts the track again. Stops it. Skips it back again. Lets it play on into the next few words – no further than 'circus sands' – and stops it.*

*He picks up the guidebook and turns to a well thumbed page, and starts to read.*

*As he does so Rick appears.*

## 3. On the cliffs above the sea.

*Waves on the rocks below. Gulls calling.*

*Rick descends and hangs in his harness in front of the rock. As he talks he will descend further, swing into the rock, and then pendule across until he reaches the far edge at the end of the speech and disappears.*

**RICK**  Scramble round the zawn and drop down to about a hundred and fifty foot above sea level. Down the groove to a sloping stance. Twenty foot. Traverse the slab. Forty foot. Left and up. Twenty foot. Climb the crack to a mantle shelf. Ninety foot. Continue left with awkward step to a chimney. Poorish rock. Fifty foot.

Below the overhangs move left on undercut holds to an open square chimney. One hundred and twenty feet. Move out left over loose, grassy rocks to the top.

Although this climb is not technically very hard, unless there's adequate protection on the final pitch there could be problems.

*Rick unclips. Disappears. The rope is pulled up and out of sight.*

**PAUL** *(Guidebook in hand)* A Dream of White Horses.

*Music loud.*

## 4. The climbing wall.

*Stevie doing squat jumps onto a small ledge, and then rising to a standing position without using her hands.*

*Paul moves in next to her and starts doing pull ups. Music fades.*

**STEVIE**   Paul...

**PAUL**   Stevie?

**STEVIE**   You can really piss me off sometimes, you know that? *(Pause)* Why can't I?

**PAUL**   Er... Because?

**STEVIE**   I'll go on my own.

**PAUL**   Go on then.

**STEVIE**   You can't stop me.

**PAUL**   I won't try.

**STEVIE**   I'll tell your mum.

**PAUL**   I'll tell yours.

**STEVIE**  Let me come, and I won't say a word.

**PAUL**  No chance.

*Stevie jumps across and steps on Paul's fingers.*

**STEVIE**  Let me.

**PAUL**  No.

**STEVIE**  Let me.

**PAUL**  No!

*She steps off his hand.*

**STEVIE**  Let me?

**PAUL**  Alright.

**STEVIE**  Yes!

*Music loud. Stevie leaps up to a ledge, followed by Paul.*

## 5. On the roof.

*Night. Traffic below.*

**PAUL**  OK?

**STEVIE**  Yeah.

*Pause.*

**STEVIE**  How do we get off?

**PAUL**  Scared?

**STEVIE**  No.

**PAUL**  We can't reverse it.

**STEVIE**  I can see that.

**PAUL**  Over to the right, round the side, and off by the fire escape.

**STEVIE**   That's on the science block.

**PAUL**   It's only a step.

**STEVIE**   A jump.

**PAUL**   If you like.

**STEVIE**   Are we going to tag it?

**PAUL**   I've already have.

**STEVIE**   Where?

**PAUL**   On the tower. By the lightning thing.

**STEVIE**   Up there?

**PAUL**   Go and have a look if you don't believe me

**STEVIE**   Alright.

*She climbs off the ledge and up into the dark, disappearing. Silence.*

*Rick appears.*

**RICK**   You sure she can do this?

**PAUL**   You know Stevie.

**RICK**   Yeah, and you know her mother too.

**PAUL**   I can't stop her. She does what she wants. *(Pause)* OK. I'll try and get her back.

Stevie... Stevie!

You fall off and we're both dead.

*Stevie returns but from the opposite side from which she left. Rick watches. He's impressed.*

**STEVIE**   You tagged it. *(She blows on her fingers and shakes them.)* I took all the skin off my fingers.

*Pause.*

**PAUL**   How did you get down?

**STEVIE**   Used the bolts on the lightning conductor.

**PAUL**   Right.

**STEVIE**   How did you do it?

**PAUL**   I had a rope. Looped it round the weather vane and abbed off.

**STEVIE**   But that was like the first ascent, and you didn't know what was up there.

**PAUL**   Yeah.

*Pause.*

*Rick disappears.*

**STEVIE**   What do we do now? Look at the view?

**PAUL**   If you want.

**STEVIE**   It's a good view.

**PAUL**   Yeah. Sometimes, if it's a warm night, I'll stay out till dawn.

**STEVIE**   How come your mum's never caught you?

**PAUL**   She has. Kind of.

**STEVIE**   How do you mean, kind of?

**PAUL**   I always come back in through the front door. She saw me once, I said I'd been out for a run.

**STEVIE**   Is she still seeing dickbrain?

**PAUL** (*He uses his mother's voice to repeat what she has said to him*) He's just a friend. I don't slag off your friends, so why do you slag off mine?

**STEVIE**   She didn't say 'slag off'.

**PAUL**   No.

**STEVIE**   Do you think she's let him?

**PAUL**   No.

**STEVIE**  You don't know.

**PAUL**  I stay up till he leaves. Even if I'm knackered.

**STEVIE**  It's been nearly three years, she might want to.

**PAUL**  I shouldn't think so.

**STEVIE**  She's not that old.

**PAUL**  I don't think she did it with my dad that much. *(Pause)* Do you want to go?

**STEVIE**  Don't mind. *(Pause)* I can see my house, but I can't see yours.

## 6. School.

*Morning. Noise. Bells. Martin standing alone. The new boy outside the office.*

*Paul enters. Stands next to him.*

**MARTIN**  You new too?

**PAUL**  What?

**MARTIN**  You new too?

**PAUL**  No.

*Pause.*

**MARTIN**  Getting done?

**PAUL**  No. *(Pause)* Missed my mark.

**MARTIN**  Why?

**PAUL**  Because I was late.

*They straighten up.*

**MARTIN**  Martin McCormack, Miss. Little c, big C. No A. In the Mc. Yeah, Miss, this morning. I wait here? OK. *(Martin* *follows the teacher.)* That kid, Miss, I don't know his name, but he wasn't properly late, he was showing me where to go. Right. Thanks Miss. *(Martin returns to Paul.)*

**MARTIN** Sorted.

**PAUL** What?

**MARTIN** You've got your mark, she doesn't want to see you.

*Paul exits, not entirely sure that he believes Martin.*

## 7. Lunchtime.

*Stevie is sitting alone. Texting.*

*Martin approaches her.*

**STEVIE** Yes?

**MARTIN** I saw you last night.

**STEVIE** Aren't you lucky.

**MARTIN** I thought you were fantastic.

**STEVIE** Yeah, I know, that's what everybody says.

**MARTIN** No, really. I was watching you through my telescope.

**STEVIE** Oh, God. A pervert.

**MARTIN** When you were climbing. On the roof. I was setting up my observatory when I saw you. I saw you both.

**STEVIE** Setting up your what?

**MARTIN** It's my bedroom really. I saw you by accident, going up the tower. I thought I'd better keep watching in case you fell off.

**STEVIE** I don't fall off.

**MARTIN** Obviously not.

**STEVIE**   Like watching people, do you?

**MARTIN**   I don't watch people. I watch stars.

**STEVIE**   You going to say anything?

**MARTIN**   No.

**STEVIE**   You best not.

**MARTIN**   I stopped watching when you went to sleep. Is that why he was late this morning? Your mate?

**STEVIE**   I don't see what it's got to do with you.

*Paul arrives.*

**PAUL**   Cheers for getting us off.

**MARTIN**   'Salright.

**STEVIE**   Don't talk to him, he's a creep.

**PAUL**   Are you a creep?

**MARTIN**   No, I'm Martin.

**PAUL**   He's not a creep.

**STEVIE**   He watches people through a telescope.

**PAUL**   Hey, cool. Do you see anything good?

**STEVIE**   Perverts. *(Stevie is texting a message to Paul.)*

**MARTIN**   Sometimes, I can't make a habit of it though, because it's in my bedroom window and people will see. But it was good at my old house.

**PAUL**   Yeah?

**MARTIN**   Yeah.

**STEVIE**   Perverts. *(Stevie exits.)*

**MARTIN**   What's up with her?

**PAUL**   Leave it, she'll be alright.

**MARTIN**  Do you want to come round? *(Paul reads the text message. It's not friendly.)* Have a go?

**PAUL**  Yeah. Why not?

**MARTIN**  It's really just stars. Mostly.

**PAUL**  OK. Just stars.

*Bell rings. They exit.*


## 8. Paul's room.


*He starts the CD. Same verse – same track – same routine.*

*Rick appears.*

**RICK**  Give it a rest, eh?

**PAUL**  Thought you liked it?

**RICK**  Over and over again? Go on. *(Paul stops the track.)* That's better.

Stevie was good last night.

**PAUL**  Yeah. *(Pause)* Don't look at me like that. I can't tell her what to do. What am I supposed to say? *(Again we hear his mother's voice going over the same argument he heard a hundred times from his bedroom)* It can't just be about you anymore, it's got to be about your family. It's not worth the risk.

**RICK**  I didn't know you'd heard us.

**PAUL**  Didn't have much choice, did I?

**RICK**  That wasn't good. Sorry. How is your mum?

**PAUL**  Alright.

**RICK**  Let her see Max.

**PAUL**  I'm not stopping her.

**RICK**     You know what I mean.

**PAUL**     You used to say he was a pillock.

**RICK**     He got on my nerves sometimes. But he's alright. He'll be good for her.

**PAUL**     He's only after one thing.

**RICK**     Maybe it's something she wants?

**PAUL**     Dad.

**RICK**     And that's not allowed because she's your mum?

**PAUL**     Don't start getting all understanding and compassionate just because you're dead. It's too late.

**RICK**     I'm only saying, that's all.

**PAUL**     Well, don't. I make you up. You're only in my head because I let you in. All I've got to do is stop thinking about you, and you'll be well screwed.

**RICK**     OK.

**PAUL**     That's the deal.

**RICK**     Right.

*Paul takes the CD out of the player and drops it. He puts in another.*

*Music loud.*

*Rick exits. Blackout.*

## 9. Martin's room.

*Martin with the telescope. Setting it up.*

*Paul appears.*

**MARTIN**  What do you want to look at?

Stupid question. I can't guarantee we'll get something, though, I haven't lived here long enough to know where to look.

Focus here and move it like this. Don't jerk it about or you won't be able to work out what you're looking at.

*Paul gets behind the telescope. He moves it around.*

**MARTIN**  Got anything?

**PAUL**  Two cats. *(He looks round the side of the telescope and then back to the lens again.)* God, you don't realise, do you? The things you're looking at are so far away. I've got Stevie's. But you wouldn't know it was hers unless you did, because you can only see the kitchen extension. Hey, I've got my house. *(Watches for a few seconds, then, not pleased with what he sees, pushes the telescope away.)*

*Pause.*

**MARTIN**  I'll show you the moon, if you want.

**PAUL**  Yeah, go on show me the moon.

**MARTIN**  You alright?

**PAUL**  Yeah, fine.

*Martin focuses the telescope.*

**MARTIN**  There. The Sea of Tranquility. That's where they landed.

**PAUL**  Who?

**MARTIN**  Who...? Peasant. Go on, look.

*Paul looks through the telescope.*

*Silence.*

**PAUL**  Bloody hell.

**MARTIN**  It's good, in it?

PAUL       It's amazing. *(Paul moves the telescope, still looking.)* And you know what all this stuff is?

MARTIN   Some of it.

PAUL       Why's it a sea if there's no water?

MARTIN   There was once. But Lunar Prospector found water ice at the south pole where it's permanently shaded.

             The exciting thing is what are they going to do with it?

PAUL       Right. I thought it was all craters?

MARTIN   There's loads of them. The one you can't see, because it's on the far side, South Pole – Aitken, is 2250km in diameter and 12km deep. That makes it the largest impact crater in the solar system.

MARTIN   Do you want the Pleiades? It's a really clear night.

PAUL       In a minute.

MARTIN   I love the names. Tranquility. Mare Vaporum. Mare Procellarum. On the far side most of the features are named after Russians, Korolev, Gagarin, Chaplygin – still they were the ones who got the first pictures.

PAUL       Climbs have good names. Vember, Ardus, The Curver, Connie's Crack.

MARTIN   Piss off.

PAUL       It's on Crafnant Crags up in the Carnedds. 160 foot. Fat Man's Chimney. Windhover. Cenotaph Corner. There's loads of them.

MARTIN   What's your favourite?

PAUL       A Dream of White Horses. *(Pause)* It's the climb my dad fell off. But I've always liked the name.

MARTIN   Was he killed?

PAUL       Yeah. About two years ago.

MARTIN   That's when my dad went.

**PAUL**    He dead too?

**MARTIN**    No, he just went. Did a lot of climbing then did he, your dad?

**PAUL**    All the time. He took me sometimes, but only easy stuff.

**MARTIN**    The other night didn't look that easy.

**PAUL**    Stevie said you saw. That was nothing. Piece of piss.

**MARTIN**    You wouldn't get me climbing a ladder.

**PAUL**    My dad did it for a living.

**MARTIN**    I didn't know you could.

**PAUL**    Oh, yeah.

**MARTIN**    You'd have to be good.

**PAUL**    He was.

**MARTIN**    How do you make a living? Climbing?

**PAUL**    Sponsorship. Adverts. Articles. Lectures. All sorts. He had his own range of climbing gear. Actually though, it wasn't all that great.

**MARTIN**    Clothes and that?

**PAUL**    No, equipment. Under his name. Krabs, nuts, descenders.

**MARTIN**    What?

**PAUL**    Stuff you use to keep you safe when you're climbing. But there were problems with the casting or something so he had to postpone the launch so when it did come out people thought it might be iffy and wouldn't touch it. After he died Mum got this massive bill. It's all sorted now.

**MARTIN**    One morning, my dad dropped me off at school, we said goodbye, I went into the playground, he drove off. Just like everyday. Only that's the last me or mum saw of him.

**PAUL**    Jesus.

**MARTIN**  We thought he'd had an accident. Then we thought he'd lost his memory. Then we thought he must be dead.

**PAUL**  And what do you think now?

**MARTIN**  That he pissed off and left us. We've had to move and everything.

**PAUL**  We moved too. But only, you know, around here.

**MARTIN**  It's a bugger when someone vanishes and you can't prove they're dead.

*Pause.*

**PAUL**  Show me them pliers, or whatever they are. *(Martin adjusts the telescope. Paul looks through.)* Sometimes I talk to my dad. In my head. I imagine him, and have conversations. It's alright except when he pisses me off.

**MARTIN**  How can he do that if you're imaging him?

**PAUL**  I don't know. Can Stevie see this, she'd really like it.

**MARTIN**  Yeah, I don't mind.

**PAUL**  Do you imagine your dad?

**MARTIN**  No way.

*Paul has let the telescope move down towards the ground.*

**PAUL**  Hey...we've got lucky!

**MARTIN**  What you mean?

**PAUL**  Tits!

*Music.*

## 10. School.

*Stevie takes out her phone. She has a text. Paul enters.*

| | |
|---|---|
| **STEVIE** | Why'd you text me when you're just about to speak to me? |
| **PAUL** | I didn't know I was. But you on tonight, though? Do the library? |
| **STEVIE** | It's only titchy. |
| **PAUL** | It's got to be done. |
| **STEVIE** | Fair enough. |
| **PAUL** | Good. Have you seen Martin? |
| **STEVIE** | No. |
| **PAUL** | Brilliant last night, wan't it? |
| **STEVIE** | Alright. |
| **PAUL** | Oh, yeah, alright, bet you've never seen anything like that before in your life. |
| **STEVIE** | I have in pictures. |
| **PAUL** | Why don't you like him? |
| **STEVIE** | I didn't say I didn't. |
| **PAUL** | You don't act like you like him. |
| **STEVIE** | Well, it's pathetic. You were both at it, and you were worse than him. I saw you. Every time you thought I wasn't looking you were swivelling that bloody telescope all over. It's creepy. I know what you looking for. |
| **PAUL** | I wasn't. |
| **STEVIE** | Wasn't what? |
| **PAUL** | Wasn't what you're saying I was. |
| **STEVIE** | Peeping Tom. |
| **PAUL** | I'm not. |
| **STEVIE** | Lads and tits. Pathetic. |
| **PAUL** | That first time at Martin's I saw my mum. Through the telescope. |

| | |
|---|---|
| **STEVIE** | Yeah? |
| **PAUL** | She was going into our house. |
| **STEVIE** | So? |
| **PAUL** | With dickbrain. |
| **STEVIE** | Is that all? |
| **PAUL** | Yeah. |
| **STEVIE** | So you're going to spy on your mum? |
| **PAUL** | No. |
| **STEVIE** | One day they might leave the curtains open and you'll catch them at it. What you going to do then? Watch? *(Paul looks as if he might hit her.)* Go on then! *(Paul exits.)* Paul! |

*Music.*


## 11. Stevie and Paul on top of a building.

*He has a rope with him.*

*Silence.*

*He gets out the spray can and tags the building.*

*Silence.*

| | |
|---|---|
| **PAUL** | I was quite happy doing this on me own, you know. You don't have to be here. |
| **STEVIE** | I said I'd come. |
| **PAUL** | Oh, speaking to me now, are you? Didn't think you talked to perverts. |

*Silence.*

**STEVIE**  I don't to even think about my mum and dad doing it, it's too gruesome. I don't think people should be allowed to have sex when they're over forty. *(Silence.)* Can I do mine?

**PAUL**  Have you got one?

**STEVIE**  Yeah. I worked it out in English.

**PAUL**  You're going to write your own name, aren't you?

**STEVIE**  No.

*Silence.*

**PAUL**  Go on then. *(He gives her the spray can. Stevie draws a much bigger tag than Paul's.)* Not that big.

**STEVIE**  Why not?

**PAUL**  People'll see it.

**STEVIE**  That's the point.

**PAUL**  Then they'll find out who we are, and we'll get done.

**STEVIE**  Never! Look at that! Right, let's go.

**PAUL**  You're in a hurry.

**STEVIE**  We've still got bags of time. I want to do the multi-storey behind Market Street.

**PAUL**  We haven't sussed it.

**STEVIE**  I have. It's simple. *(She picks up the rope. Sorts the belay and the descender. Throws it down the back of the set.)* Come on. *(She disappears.)*

*Music.*

## 12. Paul's room.

*Paul and Martin.*

*Climbing gear tumbling out of a rucksack.*

**MARTIN**  What's this?

**PAUL**  Stitch plate. Double the rope, put it through here, stick the loop in a krab, solid as a rock. Hold anybody on that with one hand. Same as the descender. Look see. Loop it through and over, safe as houses. That's for when you abb off.

**MARTIN**  Not me. I wouldn't be up there in the first place. These are good. *(Martin plays with the Friends.)*

**PAUL**  Friends.

**MARTIN**  What?

**PAUL**  What they're called, after the company that made them first.

**MARTIN**  I like these.

**PAUL**  Have a rack of them and you don't need so many nuts.

**MARTIN**  I'll believe you.

**PAUL**  Then there's slings, krabs, screwgates, all sorts.

**MARTIN**  This was all your dad's?

**PAUL**  Yeah.

**MARTIN**  But you don't use any of this stuff on the buildings?

**PAUL**  No.

**MARTIN**  You must be mad.

**PAUL**  We don't do anything we're going to fall off.

**MARTIN**  But if your dad had all this gear, how come he fell off?

**PAUL**  It was at night. He was on his own.

*Martin finds the guidebook.*

**MARTIN** *Rock Climbing in Wales.* I've got an uncle in Wales. I'm supposed to be going up there with me mum at half term. A Dream of White Horses. That's the one, is it?

**PAUL** Yeah.

**MARTIN** *(a piece of paper falls out of the book)* What's this? A poem? Did you write it?

**PAUL** It's a song.

**MARTIN** To dance beneath the diamond sky with one hand waving free?

**PAUL** He used to sing that when he was feeling good on a climb. He used to sing it all the time really, he didn't know he was doing it. Do you want to hear it? I've got it on CD.

**MARTIN** Who's singing it?

**PAUL** Dylan.

**MARTIN** No, I'm not bothered. *(Pause)* You must get frightened sometimes.

**PAUL** Didn't say I didn't. Mostly before really. Thinking about it.

**MARTIN** Have you ever been really scared? When you're up there?

**PAUL** Yeah. And you say gripped, not frightened.

**MARTIN** So have you ever been so... gripped you can't move? What's it like?

**PAUL** It's not so bad really. Your calfs shake, and because you're hanging on so hard it feels as if you're going to fall off any minute. Sometimes your head starts to whirl a bit.

**MARTIN** What do you do?

**PAUL** You focus your brain down to the size of a marble, concentrate, and don't look at or think of anything except the rock, and try to relax. Then you can start to work out what you've got to do.

**MARTIN**  What do you do if, you know, all that size of a marble stuff doesn't work?

**PAUL**  I don't know.

*Pause.*

**MARTIN**  You know Stevie?

**PAUL**  Yeah.

**MARTIN**  She fancies you.

**PAUL**  Get lost.

**MARTIN**  That's why she gets pissed off with me.

**PAUL**  Don't be stupid.

**MARTIN**  Do you fancy her though? I think she's alright. Even if she does treat me like shit half the time.

**PAUL**  I've known her since we were five.

**MARTIN**  Don't mean you can't fancy her.

*Pause.*

**PAUL**  She's gone really mental now, you know. We did the library and the multi-storey on Sunday night. Monday we sussed out the crematorium, and did it on Tuesday.

**MARTIN**  Did you tag the crematorium?

**PAUL**  No. But she's putting up her own tags now. Bloody enormous.

**MARTIN**  I know, I've seen.

**PAUL**  And you won't be the only one. There won't be much left to do soon.

**MARTIN**  She came round our house last night.

**PAUL**  Stevie?

**MARTIN**  Brought her little brother. Wanted to have a look at the telescope.

**PAUL**　　Dirty little sod.

**MARTIN**　At the moon.

**PAUL**　　Did you let him?

**MARTIN**　Yeah.

**PAUL**　　What did she do?

**MARTIN**　Talked to me mum in the kitchen.

*Pause.*

**PAUL**　　She didn't come up?

**MARTIN**　You do fancy her.

**PAUL**　　Do I bollocks.

**MARTIN**　Well, you want to get in there, cause somebody will.

**PAUL**　　You?

**MARTIN**　Me? No. She's not my type.

**PAUL**　　Who is then?

**MARTIN**　I quite fancy Mrs Hunt.

**PAUL**　　That's sick.

**MARTIN**　Why?

**PAUL**　　She must be thirty.

**MARTIN**　I know.

**PAUL**　　Go on, seriously, who do you fancy?

**MARTIN**　Seriously I fancy Suzanne Moore.

**PAUL**　　Oh so do I. Very seriously indeed. Suzanne Moore.

*Pause.*

**MARTIN**　This isn't doing me any good. Change the subject.

**PAUL**　　We've got physics tomorrow.

**MARTIN**　No good. Try again.

**PAUL**      Stevie and me are going the bridge end tower, do you want to come?

**MARTIN**  Are you mad! Oh, nice one, that's worked. You can't dwell on Suzanne Moore when you're about to shit bricks.

**PAUL**      I'm serious.

**MARTIN**  So am I.

**PAUL**      It's about the only thing round here we haven't done.

**MARTIN**  You're not getting me up there.

**PAUL**      You don't have to climb it, pillock, you can go up the stairs.

**MARTIN**  Oh, good.

**PAUL**      I've sussed it. It's open till five, so you go in, hide, and wait for us, and then you'll have the door open so we can get down.

**MARTIN**  Alarms?

**PAUL**      No.

**MARTIN**  And when are you going to climb it?

**PAUL**      About one I expect.

**MARTIN**  So I'm to sit up there for six hours. I don't think so.

**PAUL**      Please yourself.

**MARTIN**  But if I'm not there, how will you get down?

**PAUL**      Abb off. *(Pause)* I'm not sure, but I think you might be able to see Suzanne Moore's house from your bedroom window. *(Pause. And they're off like lightning.)*

*Music.*

## 13. On top of the wall.

*Paul rushes up onto the wall. Rick appears. Leaps after him. They move around the wall as they speak in a kind of chase. Music. They move in and out of light.*

| | |
|---|---|
| **RICK** | You can't do it. |
| **PAUL** | Why can't I? |
| **RICK** | You're not ready. |
| **PAUL** | Yes, I am. |
| **RICK** | I don't want you to. |
| **PAUL** | Think I'll fall? |
| **RICK** | Don't take her. |
| **PAUL** | She's coming with me. |
| **RICK** | Why does she have to go? |
| **PAUL** | I need a second. |
| **RICK** | Ask Max. |
| **PAUL** | I'm want to do it with Stevie. *(The music continues until Rick has disappeared and Paul is sitting on the top of bridge end tower.)* |

## 14. On top of the tower.

*Paul is on the top of the tower, Stevie is not yet in sight. Paul has a rope at his side.*

| | |
|---|---|
| **PAUL** | Just keep coming round. That's it. |
| **STEVIE** | I'm not keen on this. All this bird shit makes it really slippy. |
| **PAUL** | You're nearly there. |

*Stevie comes into sight.*

*She climbs up to Paul who reaches out his hand and helps her up. She is exhausted.*

**PAUL**      Interesting, wa'n it?

**STEVIE**    You could say that. *(Pause)* I thought you were supposed to have sussed this out.

**PAUL**      I did. A bit.

**STEVIE**    A bit.

**PAUL**      Most of it was alright.

**STEVIE**    It wasn't most of it I was bothered about.

**PAUL**      It was a touch manky at the top. Sorry.

**STEVIE**    It's alright. We're up here now.

*Pause.*

**PAUL**      Don't think there's much else left to do now, is there?

**STEVIE**    S'pose not.

**PAUL**      Won't do us any harm to get some proper sleep.

**STEVIE**    No.

**PAUL**      Have to think of something different to do.

**STEVIE**    Like what?

**PAUL**      I dunno... something.

**STEVIE**    Yeah.

*Silence.*

**PAUL**      Listen...

**STEVIE**    Yeah?

**PAUL**      I was wondering...

**STEVIE**    What?

**PAUL**     Do you fancy, er... you know, doing some proper routes?

**STEVIE**     What d'you mean?

**PAUL**     Multi pitch. On rock.

**STEVIE**     There's no rocks round here.

**PAUL**     We could go to Wales.

**STEVIE**     It's miles away. You and me? Go off to Wales? *(Silence)* Nobody'd let us.

**PAUL**     They might.

**STEVIE**     No.

**PAUL**     But if they did, would you?

*Pause.*

**STEVIE**     Yeah.

**PAUL**     Great, cos Martin's uncle lives in Wales and he's got this barn he rents out, and he's going up there at half term with his mum and I reckon he's working on her to let us come too.

**STEVIE**     You and me, and Martin, and his mum, and his uncle?

**PAUL**     Yeah. And there's some quarries and stuff. What d'you reckon? Will you come?

**STEVIE**     It's pretty definite?

**PAUL**     I think so.

**STEVIE**     Get his mum to ring mine, then.

**PAUL**     Excellent. And we'll go down the centre with the gear so you can get used to it all. That's brill, Stevie. Yeah.

*Pause.*

**STEVIE**     This is all so we can do your dad's climb, isn't it?

**PAUL**     That's in Anglesey. Martin's uncle lives on the mainland.

**STEVIE**     You still want us to do it though?

PAUL    Yeah.

STEVIE    Then we'll do it.

PAUL    Just like that?

STEVIE    You've planned it all, haven't you? Worked it all out?

PAUL    Yeah, I have.

STEVIE    Well, then, why not?

PAUL    Stevie...

*Pause.*

*In the distance the faint sound of a helicopter. It's been growing louder.*

STEVIE    What's that noise?

PAUL    Sounds like a helicopter. Have you got your phone?

STEVIE    Yeah.

PAUL    I'm going to ring Martin.

STEVIE    Why?

PAUL    I don't know, it just feels a bit funny.

STEVIE    Here.

PAUL    Ta. How d'you turn it on?

STEVIE    Give it here. He'll be in bed.

PAUL    No, he won't. He's probably watching us.

*The noise is getting louder.*

*He dials the number.*

PAUL    What? Are we? *(To Stevie)* We're in tonight's paper.

STEVIE    Us?

PAUL    Not us, the tagging. With pictures he says. He can see us. ... I am listening. What? ... Oh, bugger. ... Right. OK.

... Oh, cheers mate. See you. *(To Stevie)* That noise is a helicopter. It's sweeping the tops of the buildings. He reckons it's looking for us.

*The light from the helicopter moves across the set. Not yet catching them.*

**STEVIE**    You knew about the papers, didn't you?

**PAUL**    Sort of.

**STEVIE**    I'm not coming to Wales if you're going to piss about.

**PAUL**    Save it, Stevie, we've got to get off here.

**STEVIE**    What was it? See if they'd catch us?

**PAUL**    No. Come on.

**STEVIE**    If we get away with it tonight we do White Horses, if we're caught then the trip's off?

**PAUL**    Something like that.

**STEVIE**    If I do this, we do it properly. We climb it together, we come home together. I won't come if you're going to be stupid.

**PAUL**    I don't know what you mean.

**STEVIE**    Paul?

**PAUL**    Yes.

**STEVIE**    Promise.

**PAUL**    Promise.

**STEVIE**    What do we do now? We can't hide, and they'll see us if we try to abb off.

**PAUL**    Got it sorted. Martin came up and wedged the door open before they shut. He's been ringing my phone for the last hour trying to tell us.

*The light is sweeping closer.*

**STEVIE**    Come on then. *(They dive over the top.)*

**PAUL**      The rope. *(He leans over and snatches it away just as noise reaches a crescendo and the light moves onto where they were. It stays there for a moment.)*

*Blackout.*


## 15. The climbing wall.


*Stevie is sorting out the gear. Martin is helping her.*

*She puts on a harness and ties on to the rope.*

**MARTIN**  He's late.

**STEVIE**   You'll do till he gets here.

**MARTIN**  Thanks.

**STEVIE**   Clip that sling on there for a belay. That's it. Now the stitch plate. That one.

**MARTIN**  I know what to do. I've watched enough times. *(He prepares the belay.)* OK, I'm ready if you are.

**STEVIE**   Say climb when you're ready.

**MARTIN**  You are ready.

**STEVIE**   Say it.

**MARTIN**  Climb when you're ready.

**STEVIE**   Climbing.

*Pause.*

**MARTIN**  Go on then.

**STEVIE**   Before I start you have to say 'OK'.

**MARTIN**  Why? I can see you're OK. You're right in front of me.

**STEVIE**     And if I'm out of sight? What then? You've got to get the signals right, Martin.

**MARTIN**     OK. That was me agreeing with you, and getting the signals right.

*Stevie starts to climb. The rope loops down behind her as she crosses the rock.*

**STEVIE**     Take in.

**MARTIN**     Sorry.

**STEVIE**     Not that much. Right, I'm up.

*She has stopped halfway across the wall. She starts to rig a belay.*

**MARTIN**     No, you're not.

**STEVIE**     We're turning this into a two pitch climb. For practice.

**MARTIN**     What does that mean?

**STEVIE**     You're coming up too.

**MARTIN**     No way.

**STEVIE**     Martin, stop being such a wimp and put that harness on. *(He does as he's told, but slowly.)* Hurry up.

**MARTIN**     If I take my time, Paul might arrive and then he can do it.

**STEVIE**     You're doing it.

               Taking in. *(Prompts him)* 'That's me.'

**MARTIN**     That's me.

**STEVIE**     Climb when you're ready.

**MARTIN**     Climbing.

**STEVIE**     OK. *(Nothing happens.)* Get a move on, you big lump.

**MARTIN**     Is that one of the signals? I'm not really keen on this. *(Stevie yanks the rope and he starts to climb. He is not a natural climber.)*

**STEVIE**     You're doing great.

**MARTIN**  I don't want to look down.

**STEVIE**  You're only just off the ground.

**MARTIN**  It doesn't feel like it.

**STEVIE**  And don't hug the rock, lean out.

**MARTIN**  If I want to hug it, I'll hug it.

**STEVIE**  It's easier if you don't.

*He arrives at the stance.*

**MARTIN**  Is that it? Can I go down now?

**STEVIE**  This is the bit where I put my life in your hands and finish the route. Don't worry, I'm not going to fall off. *(Stevie gets Martin into the rope system.)*

**MARTIN**  He's told me about his dad, Paul, what he was like and that. And I know it was after dark when he did this White Horses thing, and he was on his own, but he was really good, wasn't he? And he'd done the climb loads of times apparently...

**STEVIE**  Do you mean, did he jump?

**MARTIN**  Kind of...

**STEVIE**  Paul doesn't know for sure. Nobody does.

**MARTIN**  But...?

**STEVIE**  He might have done, yes. Don't tell him I said so, will you?

**MARTIN**  No. You've got to think about what might have happened.

**STEVIE**  Like with your dad?

**MARTIN**  You try not to after a bit.

**STEVIE**  I don't think he jumped.

**MARTIN**  You trust him, don't you? Paul.

**STEVIE**   I wouldn't trust him not to nick my homework and hand it in as his, but when we're climbing, yeah, I trust him. And he's got to trust me too.

**MARTIN**   Nothing's going to happen is it? You and Paul. Up there.

**STEVIE**   No. Nothing's going to happen. Come on, let's get on with it.

**MARTIN**   Oh, shit.

**STEVIE**   What?

**MARTIN**   I'd forgotten where we were. Can I get down?

**STEVIE**   No. *(Paul arrives as they are going through the drill and Stevie moves off the stance. He watches them. Stevie gets to the top, quickly fixes the belay.)* OK.

*Martin leaves the stance with great reluctance.*

**PAUL**   I never thought I'd see this.

**MARTIN**   Neither did I.

**PAUL**   Don't hug the–

**MARTIN**   She's already told me.

**PAUL**   Doesn't listen, does he?

*Martin grinds to a halt.*

**MARTIN**   Look, I'm not messing about, I don't think I can go any further. Up or down. My legs are shaking.

**PAUL**   Come on, you can do it.

**MARTIN**   I can't. Honestly, I can't.

*Paul has slipped a pair of climbing slippers on. He climbs up to Martin.*

**PAUL**   Stevie's got you, so you can't fall off.

**MARTIN**   I want to go down.

**PAUL**   It's going to be easier to go up then go down.

**MARTIN**  No, it isn't.

**PAUL**  Come on. Lift your leg up, and then take hold... *(Paul directs and supports, bullies and coaxes him to the top. When he gets there he flops down exhausted. After a moment he picks himself up. Stevie and Paul sort out the gear.)*

**STEVIE**  Well done.

**MARTIN**  Well done? I was bricking myself.

**PAUL**  You did it.

**MARTIN**  But from now on I watch, yeah?

**STEVIE**  If you're sure...?

**MARTIN**  Bugger off. I've sorted Anglesey. There's no need for us to take off on our own.

**PAUL**  How come?

**MARTIN**  Mum'll take us. I'll have my telescope and camera with me, so that's OK. I want to go to the cliffs for the birds and that.

**STEVIE**  You're a bird watcher?

**MARTIN**  Yes?

**STEVIE**  Nothing.

**PAUL**  What about us?

**MARTIN**  You want to explore round the bottom of the cliffs, and look at the caves. You'll get the lecture about not getting caught by the tide, but that's all. She'll never dream you're going right to the top.

**PAUL**  We need to be there for two days. We've got to suss it out. We'll need your telescope.

**MARTIN**  Don't worry, I'll work it.

**PAUL**  Brilliant. Fancy a go at the end wall, Stevie?

**STEVIE**  Sure. You want to lead?

**MARTIN**  I'm not doing it.

**PAUL**  No, you're not, it's a 6b.

**MARTIN**  Oh, right. So what grade was this then?

**STEVIE**  It doesn't really have a grade, Martin.

**MARTIN**  Why not?

**PAUL**  It's a bit too easy.

*Paul and Stevie start to climb down. Within seconds they're on the floor.*

**MARTIN**  Excuse me.

**PAUL**  Yeah?

**MARTIN**  How am I supposed to get down?

*Music.*

*Blackout.*

## 16. Paul's room.

*Rick sitting.*

*Paul sorting and packing gear.*

**RICK**  Up for it?

**PAUL**  Yeah.

**RICK**  Mum know?

**PAUL**  She knows I'm taking the gear. She knows we'll be climbing.

**RICK**  But she doesn't know what?

**PAUL**  No.

**RICK**  Do you think she's guessed? Should you tell her?

**PAUL**    No. We can do it. We've got the gear, we've got the experience.

**RICK**    On rock?

**PAUL**    Yeah, not on rock, but we'll be fine.

**RICK**    You sure you're happy about Stevie?

**PAUL**    Oh, yeah. Positive. Come on, dad, it's a trade route.

**RICK**    It's not a trade route. It's a classic.

**PAUL**    We're going to do this.

**RICK**    Fair enough, go ahead.

*Pause.*

**PAUL**    You don't mind?

**RICK**    No.

**PAUL**    It's your route.

**RICK**    It's anybody's route.

**PAUL**    When you... where exactly did it happen?

**RICK**    Do you really need to know?

**PAUL**    No. *(Goes back to his gear.)*

**RICK**    Don't forget, if it feels good, you're allowed to sing.

*Pause.*

**PAUL**    Dad?

*Paul turns, but his father has gone.*

*He packs the rucksack and then leaves.*

*Blackout.*

*Music.*

## 17. On the beach.

*Paul, Stevie, and Martin.*

*Walking across the beach.*

*Stevie is barefoot, carrying her trainers. They reach the point where the climb comes into view and look up.*

**STEVIE**    Is that it?

**PAUL**    That's it.

**MARTIN**    It's much too big. You can't go up there.

**STEVIE**    Can we see the start from here?

**PAUL**    Almost, it's tucked behind that nose.

**MARTIN**    What nose?

**PAUL**    There look. About a third of the way up. See, we don't have to climb it all.

**MARTIN**    But how do you get up there?

**PAUL**    We come down off the big zawn and work our way round.

**MARTIN**    But that means you've got to go down almost as far as you go up before you start. Bloody hell.

**STEVIE**    Martin. Shut up.

**MARTIN**    Sorry.

**STEVIE**    Depends how long it's going to take. Is it worth going up and having a look?

**PAUL**    We haven't got time to go all the way up and round, and I'm not sure how much we'd see anyway. I reckon we'll learn more from down here.

**MARTIN**    Where will I be?

**STEVIE**    On the beach sunbathing?

**MARTIN**    I want to take pictures.

**PAUL**      We've got a spare rope, you could abb off the top. Get some really good close ups.

**MARTIN**      I don't think so. Anyway, I've got a telephoto lens.

**STEVIE**      Lucky you.

**PAUL**      What about up there?

**MARTIN**      On that big lump? Is it solid?

**STEVIE**      As a rock.

**PAUL**      There's a path, and a viewpoint thing. You'll be fine.

**MARTIN**      I didn't know you'd been here before.

**STEVIE**      Neither did I.

**PAUL**      Me and mum came on our own. We didn't come down here though, the tide was in. Get your telescope out then.

*Martin sets up the telescope. Paul watches him. Stevie paddles.*

**MARTIN**      There you go.

*Paul looks through the telescope.*

**PAUL**      Stevie? *(Stevie walks across to have a look.)* Got it?

**STEVIE**      Yeah. *(She studies the route, Paul beside her. Martin has taken his camera out. He takes a picture of her.)* It's all there, isn't it?

**PAUL**      Yep.

**STEVIE**      Well, that's the main thing. *(Martin has moved away, concentrating on his camera.)* It's pretty much as I thought it would be. Overhang could be interesting. Especially if we're knackered.

**PAUL**      What d'you reckon?

**STEVIE**      It's OK.

**PAUL**      You sure about this?

**STEVIE**      I'm sure.

**PAUL**  Good.

*Stevie moves to let Paul look again. She sits on the sand. Martin is taking pictures of the cliffs. He turns, sees her, walks across. She smiles and poses for him. He sits next to her, sorts through his bag for a lens case. Finds what he wants. Gets up.*

**MARTIN**  I'll be down there.

**STEVIE**  See you in a bit.

*Martin exits.*

*Paul is still studying the route. Stevie gets up and sits next to him.*

**PAUL**  We can do this.

**STEVIE**  Course we can.

**PAUL**  Alternate leads?

**STEVIE**  Of course.

**PAUL**  You scared?

**STEVIE**  Me? No. I do stuff like that everyday before breakfast.

**PAUL**  We don't have to do it.

**STEVIE**  We only do what we want to do.

**PAUL**  No moaning, no whinging, if one of us doesn't want to do it, it's off.

**STEVIE**  It's always worked before.

**PAUL**  When I think about it, I can see us both at the top.

**STEVIE**  Yeah. So can I.

**PAUL**  Where's he gone?

**STEVIE**  Down there somewhere.

**PAUL**  Do you want to go and get a feel of the rock, or something?

**STEVIE**  No. Stay here, eh?

*Stevie gets up. So does Paul. She wants to put on her trainers, but her feet are covered with sand. She puts one hand on Paul's shoulder to support herself while she wipes her feet off. On the second trainer she loses her balance slightly and Paul puts out an arm to support her. When she has both trainers on they stand close to each other, still touching. Looking up at the climb.*

**STEVIE**　We'd better make a move.

**PAUL**　I suppose so.

**STEVIE**　Have we seen enough?

**PAUL**　Everything we're going to from down here.

**STEVIE**　All down to tomorrow, then.

**PAUL**　It might rain. We might forget the rope. Anything could happen between now and then. My dad once went all the way to Cornwall with Max and neither of them realised they hadn't got a rope until they were at the bottom of the cliffs.

**STEVIE**　It's not going to rain, and we won't forget the rope. I'll go and round up, bird boy. *(She exits.)*

*Paul starts to put the telescope away and pack up the rest of the stuff.*

**PAUL**　Dad? *(He carries on with what he's doing. Then stops and looks around.)* Dad? *(Pause)* Typical.

*Music.*

*Blackout.*

## 18. Martin's stance. Up high.

*Paul, Stevie, and Martin. They have the bag with his cameras and his telescope. They are behind their schedule.*

**MARTIN**  It's not my fault. If we'd told my mum we wanted to come up here she'd have got suspicious.

**STEVIE**  Three miles we've had to lug this stuff.

**PAUL**  It doesn't matter. Are we still doing the route?

**STEVIE**  Yes.

**PAUL**  Then let's concentrate on that, yeah? *(They dump Martin's stuff.)* Now, you OK?

**MARTIN**  I'll be fine.

**PAUL**  The finish is over there, so, if you've got enough bottle, you can come across and meet us.

**MARTIN**  I think I'll wave from here.

**PAUL**  We're going to go back and pick up our stuff, so the next time you'll see us we should be somewhere down there.

**MARTIN**  Have you got your phones?

**PAUL**  Yeah, but they won't be switched on.

**MARTIN**  See you then.

**PAUL**  See you.

**STEVIE**  Bye.

**MARTIN**  Good luck.

*They exit. Martin waits till they're out of sight and then takes the rope he's been given and disappears. He returns with it tied round his waist and trailing behind him. It's not long enough for him to get to his gear, so he has to go back and readjust it.*

*He sorts his stuff out and settles down as near to the edge as he dares.*

## 19. On the climb.

*Below Martin. Stevie and Martin on the stance.*

**STEVIE**    How long have we been going?

**PAUL**    'Bout a couple of hours. It's tight, but we're doing fine. Enjoying it?

**STEVIE**    It's brilliant. You?

**PAUL**    Yeah.

**STEVIE**    Right, my turn. Up there and across?

**PAUL**    You got it.

**STEVIE**    Climbing.

**PAUL**    OK.

*Stevie starts to climb.*

## 20. Martin's stance.

*He's watching through the telescope.*

**MARTIN**    And after a brief pause on the stance Stevie Pits leads through. Both these climbers have absolute trust in each other. And they are making excellent time on this most challenging of routes. *(He comes away from the telescope and looks at his watch.)* Actually they're not. Pretty good time, but not excellent. *(He goes back to the telescope.)* So fluid are her movements, so easy does she make it look, it's as if she and the rock are at one. *(Stevie falls.)* Shit!

## 21. Stevie hanging from the rope a few feet below her protection.

**PAUL**    Stevie! Stevie!

**STEVIE**    It's alright, I'm OK. I'm fine. Thanks for that.

**PAUL**    Just relax. 've got you.

**STEVIE**    Glad you were awake.

**PAUL**    What happened?

**STEVIE**    Nothing really. I just got careless, I think. I had a jam in, and it felt bomb proof. But obviously it wasn't.

**PAUL**    Take your time.

**STEVIE**    Yeah, I will.

*Pause.*

**PAUL**    Do you want to reverse it and I'll take over? Give you a rest?

**STEVIE**    No, I'm fine. Just cross with myself. Right, I'm back on.

**PAUL**    I've got you.

*Stevie climbs up to the stance and fixes the belay.*

**STEVIE**    I'm there.

## 22. Martin's stance.

*He's got a drink in his hand and he's stuffing a Mars bar.*

**MARTIN**    Oh, Jesus. If that's going to happen all the time I can't watch. *(He takes his camera and tries to focus it. He puts it down.)* My hands are shaking. *(He holds his hands out, fingers spread, studying them. Next he feels his forehead. Then tries to find his pulse. He can't in either his neck or in wrist, so he feels around his chest. Checking it against* *his watch.)* And I'm only watching. *(He goes back to the telescope.)* Come on, don't hang about, we don't want it getting dark.

## 23. On the climb.

*On the stance. Paul is getting out chocolate and a stig bottle.*

**PAUL**      Here.

**STEVIE**   We should get on.

**PAUL**      We're doing fine. Have some.

*They pass the bottle between them, then start on the chocolate.*

**STEVIE**   Sorry.

**PAUL**      Doesn't matter, it was only a slip. And that's what all this stuff's for. At least we know it works now.

**STEVIE**   I feel stupid.

**PAUL**      Don't, it's my fault, I started us rushing everything. And that's when things happen. We slow it down. Enjoy it. We'll get there just as fast.

*Paul puts the bottle away.*

**PAUL**      Don't do it again, though, you've probably given Martin a heart attack as it is.

**STEVIE**   Should we wave or something?

**PAUL**      No, don't do that, he'll get the wrong idea and get the rescue out.

**STEVIE**   Yeah. *(Pause)* You ready now?

**PAUL**      If you are.

**STEVIE**   Yeah, let's get going.

**PAUL**      But, slowly and carefully.

**STEVIE**   Slowly and carefully.

**PAUL**     Climbing.

**STEVIE**   OK.

*Paul starts to climb.*

## 24. Martin's stance.

**MARTIN**   You think they'd wave or something. Miserable buggers. At least they're off again. *(His phone rings. He searches for it, snatches it up.)* Yes! Oh, Mum. No, fine. No, nothing, I thought you were someone else. Just somebody who wasn't you. I'm not being mysterious. What do you want, mother? Meet you at the station not the beach? No problem, we'll be there. Me? Looking at the view. Oh, they're messing about on the rocks. *(Shouts)* It's my Mum! *(Back to the phone)* They're waving. *(He starts to make crackling noises)* You're breaking up, I can't hear you. *(He makes one last crackling noise and turns the phone off, then goes back to the telescope.)* What are they doing now? *(He eats a sandwich while watching.)* Oh, hell, I think he's stuck. *(Martin edges back out of sight.)*

## 25. On the climb.

*Stevie is belaying. Paul is out off her line of sight. He's not moving, and hasn't been for some time.*

*It's edging towards the end of the afternoon. Not dark, but less light, just enough to heighten the focus on Paul.*

**STEVIE**   Paul?

**PAUL**     Yeah?

**STEVIE**   You alright?

**PAUL**     Just having a breather.

**STEVIE**   Take as long as you like. *(Paul doesn't move. Stevie gets out some chocolate without losing hold of the belay.)* Is it a bit tricky?

**PAUL**     A bit. Just need to concentrate.

**STEVIE**   I'll shut up. *(She looks out at the view. Her fingers alert to any movement on the rope.)*

*Paul tries to move up, she responds, but he hasn't got the confidence to carry the move through and backs down. She responds. She's relaxed, over her fall, and she's confident he'll solve the problem, and she's content to wait until he does.*

*Paul is going nowhere. He knows it. He's stuck by a nut and he hasn't got the confidence to leave it and make the crux move.*

*We hear Rick's voice.*

**RICK**     To dance between the diamond sky, with one hand waving free...

**PAUL**     I'm not dancing, Dad, I'm stuck.

*Rick appears and climbs down to him.*

**RICK**     You look a bit gripped.

**PAUL**     I can't do it, Dad. I could ten minutes ago, but I can't now.

**RICK**     You have to let go, and trust your feet.

**PAUL**     I know what I've got to do, it's doing it.

*Rick checks the belay.*

**RICK**     You're rock solid there. Stevie won't let you fall.

**PAUL**     I don't want to fall.

**RICK**     Yeah, it's not all it's cracked up to be. Come on, I've seen you do harder things than this.

**PAUL**     I know. But I can't.

| | |
|---|---|
| **RICK** | Look. Take one hand off and give your arm a good shake. You can do that. *(Paul does so.)* Now the other one. That's it. Now, one leg at a time, if you can, make yourself relax. And breathe properly, stop panting. *(Paul appears to relax a little.)* |
| **PAUL** | I still can't move. |
| **RICK** | That's OK, there's no rush. How's your mum? When's Max going to move in? |
| **PAUL** | What! |
| **RICK** | Thought if I changed the subject it might help. |
| **PAUL** | Well, it doesn't. And stop pissing me about. I'm the one stuck up here, not you, you just can just step into space anytime you want and nothing's going to happen to you cause it already has. |
| **RICK** | It's not such a big deal being dead, I don't recommend you try it any sooner than you need to, but once you've done it, well, you'll see what I mean. |
| **PAUL** | Is that what's going to happen? |
| **RICK** | Don't be silly, how can it? The pair of you can hang there all night, the rescue'll get you in the morning. If you want to do yourself an injury you'll have to untie and jump off. |
| **PAUL** | At least I wouldn't be stuck here terrified. |
| **RICK** | All you've got to do is let go, stand up, reach round, and you're away. |
| **PAUL** | I can't! |
| **RICK** | Have you tried? |

*Pause.*

| | |
|---|---|
| **PAUL** | You jumped, didn't you ? Because of mum, the money, everything? |
| **RICK** | Me? |

**PAUL**    Yeah. You bottled out, just like me.

**RICK**    You're right about the money. And mum. And you'll have worked out for yourself that the climbing was coming to an end. No future there. But I didn't jump.

**PAUL**    No?

**RICK**    No. This was my favourite. I didn't even mind when Ed Drummond put it up and beat me to it. It was a beautiful night. The sea was calm, there was a full moon shining on the water, bright as day. I came up here to say goodbye. I was going to jack it in. I'd seen this old barn. We could afford it. I was going to persuade you and your mum to sell the house, come up here and open it for climbers and walkers. But make it comfortable, as well as cheap. I was ahead of my time.

**PAUL**    So what happened?

**RICK**    Too relaxed. Mind on other things. I was on automatic pilot, climbing really well, playing through in my head all the things I was going to say to you both, how you were going to react, what the future was going to be like. I remember I was actually chuckling away to myself over something or other when I lost it.

**PAUL**    But that's not fair.

**RICK**    Lesson number one. Who said it had to be fair? Still, doesn't matter, someone else bought the barn. He's done it up well, hasn't he?

**PAUL**    Martin's uncle?

**RICK**    That's the one. Come on, you've been here long enough. *(He leans out away from the rock facing down and takes both of Paul's hands and lifts them off the rock placing them where they should go. He straightens up and moves to the side to let Paul past.)* There you go, you can finish it on your own. Alright now.

**PAUL**    Thanks Dad.

**RICK**  And watch the finish, it's a bit manky. *(Rick disappears and Paul continues to climb. Stevie plays out the rope. Unconcerned, he's solved the problem.)*

*Paul arrives at the top. Stands. Looks around, then disappears to sort out a belay. When he's in the system, he shouts for Stevie.*

**PAUL**  Stevie!

**STEVIE**  Yeah!

**PAUL**  Cracked it!

**STEVIE**  Excellent.

**PAUL**  You ready?

**STEVIE**  Yeah.

**PAUL**  Taking in.

**STEVIE**  That's me.

**PAUL**  Climb when you're ready.

**STEVIE**  Climbing.

*From behind him comes a groan. Martin crawls on to the top clutching his rope.*

**MARTIN**  You've done it.

**PAUL**  What are you doing here?

**MARTIN**  I thought you were stuck.

**PAUL**  Got a bit gripped, that's all. Just out of curiosity, if I had been stuck, what were you going to do?

**MARTIN**  I've no idea.

*Stevie appears.*

**STEVIE**  What are you doing up here?

**MARTIN**  Don't ask.

| | |
|---|---|
| **STEVIE** | Nice one, Paul. Thought we might have had a bit of an epic there for a moment or too. |
| **PAUL** | Yeah. So did I. Come on, let's get going before Martin's mum gets her knickers in a twist. |

*They pack up and leave. Supporting Martin who won't even look over the edge.*

## 26. Top of science block.

*School sounds below.*

*Martin is checking the contents of one of those white boxes that have weather gauges etc in them.*

*Stevie and Paul are looking at the view.*

| | |
|---|---|
| **STEVIE** | Done that one and that one and that one. |
| **PAUL** | What we should have done is the fire station tower. |
| **MARTIN** | Oh, what a good idea. |
| **STEVIE** | Do you want to? |
| **PAUL** | No. What you doing tonight, Martin? |
| **MARTIN** | Me? |
| **STEVIE** | Yeah, you. |
| **MARTIN** | Do you really want to know? |
| **PAUL** | No. |
| **STEVIE** | I do. Tell me. |
| **MARTIN** | I am going to the pictures, and maybe on to a club. |
| **STEVIE** | With? |
| **MARTIN** | Suzanne Moore. |

*Stevie looks at Paul to see if there's any reaction. There isn't. Just.*

**PAUL**     Hope you have a good night.

**MARTIN**   So do I. In fact Suzanne and I have arranged to meet this lunchtime, as soon as she's finished her aerobics. So I have places to be. See you guys later.

*Martin exits.*

**PAUL**     What shall we do tonight then?

*Pause.*

**STEVIE**   Stop in?

**PAUL**     Yeah. Good idea.

*As they exit Rick appears.*

**RICK**     Unless there is adequate protection on the final pitch there could be problems...

**PAUL**     Piss off, Dad.

**STEVIE**   What did you say?

**PAUL**     Nothing.

*They exit as Rick watches.*

*Blackout. Music. Lights.*

*Rick, Stevie and Paul abb down to the stage. They look around for Martin, and he descends like a rocket from the highest point of all.*

*Play out to 'Heroes' by Bowie.*

*The end.*

# BIRDBOY

*Birdboy* was first produced in an Action Transport / Nottingham Playhouse Roundabout Company co-production and opened on 25th January 2005.

Directed by Kevin Dyer.

## Characters

| | |
|---|---|
| Tim | Gareth Cooper |
| Eddie | Paul Dodds |
| Ron, Tim's dad | Tim Barton |
| Tim's mum | Cerianne Roberts |

### 1.

*On the Knoll. Eddie enters. He goes to his hiding place and takes out a roll of cloth. Inside is a long, battered piece of metal with a makeshift handle. Caradoc's sword. He holds the sword in both hands, above his head, pointing to the floor behind him. He swings round to face two imaginary opponents. He defeats them both, twisting, turning, leaping from side to side. Finally he performs a set routine of strokes with the sword, before bringing it down swiftly and holding it out, rigid in front of him. He lowers the sword, and replaces it in its hiding place.*

*Eddie exits.*

## 2.

*A stone is kicked on stage. Tim enters, following the stone. Tim plays with it, then as he kicks it ahead of him, Eddie enters, sees Tim, and puts his foot on the stone. Tim doesn't know what to do. He decides to keep going, and leave the stone behind.*

**EDDIE**     Where you off?

**TIM**        Hello, Faker.

**EDDIE**     Why aren't you at school?

**TIM**        We got inset. *(The bus can be heard arriving and coming to a halt.)* That's your bus, in it?

**EDDIE**     So?

**TIM**        They'll go without you.

**EDDIE**     No they won't. Hey, be your bus in September. When you come up to the comp. And I'll be there, waiting for you. Be nice to see a friendly face, won't it? *(Eddie flicks the stone back to Tim as he walks back to the bus stop.)* Something for you to look forward to.

*Tim watches him go.*

**TIM**        I'm not going to that school. I am never going to that school. If I can kick this stone all the way to the shop, without it going in the gutter once, my dad'll be transferred to another job and we'll move house before September and I won't have to.

               If I can kick this stone all the way to the river... Faker'll do something really bad today and get expelled.

               If I can kick this stone all the way to the river and skim it four times and make it jump the rock in front of the second arch Faker'll get run over and die!

*Tim puts the stone down to kick it to the river. Mum enters.*

| | |
|---|---|
| **MUM** | Where are you going? |
| **TIM** | School. |
| **MUM** | I thought it was an inset day. |
| **TIM** | They changed it. I told you. |
| **MUM** | You're supposed to be going to gran's. Dad's waiting for you. |
| **TIM** | I've got school. |
| **MUM** | I could write a note, say you're poorly? It's only the last day. |
| **TIM** | I can't. |
| **MUM** | I was sure you'd finished yesterday. |

*Tim's Dad enters.*

| | |
|---|---|
| **DAD** | He doesn't want to miss his last day. You've obviously got it wrong. |
| **TIM** | Hi, Dad. Can I go please, Mum? |
| **MUM** | Yes, see you later. *(Tim watches and listens as they walk away.)* I could have sworn he finished yesterday. |
| **DAD** | Can we get a move on, please? |
| **MUM** | We should have found him another school. |
| **DAD** | I thought we'd tried. |
| **MUM** | There's still time before September. |
| **TIM** | No way. |
| **DAD** | Going private isn't really an option... |
| **MUM** | You said we could manage. |
| **DAD** | ...and what's the point of sending him somewhere nearly forty miles away? He'll spend half his life on a bus. Didn't we agree to wait and how he gets on? |
| **TIM** | I wish you'd both shut up and leave me alone. |

*He kicks the stone off in frustration and exits.*

MUM     Something's worrying him, and it's more than just going to a new school.

DAD     If it was anything important, he'd tell us.

MUM     It's too much bother, isn't it?

DAD     What is?

MUM     If it's not about your precious work, you're not interested. Our son is obviously unhappy...

DAD     And I'm very concerned, but I'm also very late, so can we talk about this tonight, eh?

MUM     Of course, whatever you say. *(Mum exits, Dad follows.)*

## 3.

*Tim comes on stage in a clean shirt and school trousers. Mum enters to get him ready for his first day.*

MUM     Come on, you haven't got time to stand about doing nothing. *(She pulls him a school sweat shirt over his head. He struggles into it, and she fills a new school bag with the things she has bought him.)* Can't have you being late on your first day. You do look smart. Right. New pen. New pencils. Geometry set. Notebook. Felts. Have I forgotten anything? *(She gives him the bag.)* Dinner money. Here. And I've put something in your bag for break. Is there anything else you need?

TIM     No.

MUM     Are you excited?

TIM     No.

MUM     It won't be as bad as you think. Everybody's a bit nervous on the first day.

*Tim is left on his own in his new school playground. He isn't sure where he's supposed to be. He takes a map of the school and a timetable out of his pocket and tries to work out where he is. Eddie enters.*

**EDDIE**  You're lost, aren't you?

**TIM**  No.

**EDDIE**  What's your next lesson?

**TIM**  It's...

*Eddie takes the timetable from him.*

**EDDIE**  Science. And where's the science block? *(Eddie puts his arm around Tim's shoulders, and stands looking at the map as if he's telling him where to go.)* You're going to love this place. They'll take your dinner money, put your head down the toilet... *(Tim tries to leave.)* Where you going?

**TIM**  Leave me alone, Faker.

**EDDIE**  I can't. I have to stay here all break, if any year seven student is in difficulty, I'm here to answer their questions and give them a helping hand. You're in difficulty, aren't you?

**TIM**  No.

**EDDIE**  Oh, yes, you are. Ask me a question.

**TIM**  Is your dad going to be on *Millionaire*?

This kid said your dad had got through to the final finger on *Millionaire*.

**EDDIE**  Yeah, he has.

**TIM**  When's he going to be on?

**EDDIE**  Sometime in October if they can fit him in.

**TIM**      That's brilliant. They take you down first class on the train and put you in this dead posh hotel, and you can go too...

**EDDIE**    Shut up and ask me a proper question!

**TIM**      I don't need any help.

**EDDIE**    Well, you're going to get it. And smile! Cos I'm being watched. Now, if you don't help me demonstrate that I can be a responsible member of the school community, sensitive to the needs of others, I'm going to thump you, right? Open your nice new bag.

*Tim opens his bag, and holds it so that Eddie can reach inside.*

**EDDIE**    Pencil case. Homework Diary. Books. Ah.

*Eddie finds the fruit bar Tim's mother has put in for break, and eats it.*

**EDDIE**    Apricot, almonds and yoghurt? Why can't you have a Mars bar like somebody normal? What else you got?

**TIM**      Nothing.

**EDDIE**    Let's see, shall we?

*Eddie searches through the bag, and finds Tim's book about Caradoc. He takes it out, and flicks through it.*

**TIM**      That's...

**EDDIE**    I know what it is. Where d'you get it?

**TIM**      Mrs Adams gave it me when I left. I was in her class.

**EDDIE**    So was I. I had something really brilliant planned for you, but it'll have to wait. But nothing's changed. Remember that.

**TIM**      Give me my book back.

*Eddie smiles at Tim and points.*

**EDDIE**    The science block's through there, and up the second set of stairs. Make sure you tell your teacher how helpful I was.

## 4.

*At Eddie's house.*

*Eddie is reading the book he's taken from Tim. He starts to copy one of the drawings of Caradoc on top of a hill, sword in hand, into an exercise book. His father comes in.*

**RON**    You doing homework? Bloody hell.

*Eddie covers up what he's drawing.*

**RON**    Please yourself.

**EDDIE**    Go on then, if you want. *(Eddie hands him the book. Ron looks at the drawings.)*

**RON**    Who's this, then?

**EDDIE**    Caradoc.

**RON**    Never heard of him.

**EDDIE**    He was the last British king before the Romans.

**RON**    What's so special about him then?

**EDDIE**    They couldn't defeat him. He was brilliant, like... SAS. He'd get behind their lines, hit 'em hard, then vanish. Eight years he had them on the run.

**RON**    But they got him in the end?

**EDDIE**    It wasn't his fault though. He made like he was running away, but he was leading them into this trap...

**RON**    Custer's Last Stand.

**EDDIE**    Yeah. But then things went wrong, and he escaped, and...

| | |
|---|---|
| **RON** | Where'd all this happen then? |
| **EDDIE** | Up on the Knoll. There used to be a fort up there and everything... |
| **RON** | So how'd they get him then? |
| **EDDIE** | He had this agreement with this queen that she'd protect him, but she betrayed him and sent him back to the Romans, and... |
| **RON** | Have you put the tea on? |
| **EDDIE** | Not yet. I haven't had time. |
| **RON** | How long does it take to stick a ready meal in the oven? *(Ron goes to leave.)* |
| **EDDIE** | Dad... |
| **RON** | My name's Ron. |
| **EDDIE** | This kid said you'd got through the phone calls to the fastest finger on *Millionaire*. |
| **RON** | He's lying. |
| **EDDIE** | He reckons you told his dad. |
| **RON** | I might have said I'd phoned up to try and get on. |
| **EDDIE** | Did yer? |
| **RON** | Course not. |
| **EDDIE** | Then why say you have? |
| **RON** | Cos it's a laugh. Get the tea on. *(Ron exits.)* |

## 5.

*At Tim's house.*

| | |
|---|---|
| **MUM** | How did it go then? |
| **DAD** | Survive, did you? |

| | |
|---|---|
| **MUM** | Were the teachers nice? |
| **DAD** | He's fine, look at him. |
| **MUM** | Did anyone pick on you? |
| **TIM** | I'm OK. |
| **MUM** | You sure? |
| **TIM** | Nobody picked on me. |
| **MUM** | You promise. |
| **DAD** | Anna, you heard. Nobody picked on him. Here you go, Tim. *(Dad gives Tim a present – an iPhone or other recent fashionable electronic device, but not the very latest model. Tim unwraps it, dropping the paper.)* |
| **TIM** | Thanks, Dad. |
| **DAD** | Special day, and all that. Right, I'm off. |
| **MUM** | Where are you going? |
| **DAD** | Work... |
| **MUM** | At this time? |
| **DAD** | Can't be helped. |
| **MUM** | I thought we were all eating together tonight. |
| **DAD** | Something's come up. |
| **MUM** | I wish you'd let me know when something comes up. |
| **DAD** | Don't start, Anna. See you later, Tim. *(Dad exits.)* |
| **TIM** | I've already got an iPhone, he brought me one back from Singapore. |
| **MUM** | It's the thought that counts, love. Well, there's nothing to stop us having something to eat. I did Chicken Kiev, specially, come on, you can tell me all about today. |
| **TIM** | I thought I might go out for a bit. Can I have mine later? *(Tim exits. Mum picks up the wrapping paper, and exits.)* |

# 6.

*Music.*

*Tim goes to the Knoll. He climbs onto the rock. He stretches out his arms and takes off. As he soars and dips Eddie comes out and watches him for a moment before he grabs him and forces him to the ground, his hands over Tim's eyes.*

**EDDIE**   Who is it?

**TIM**   Get off me!

**EDDIE**   Who is it?

**TIM**   I don't care! Get off.

*Eddie pushes him face down and puts his foot between his shoulder blades.*

**EDDIE**   It's me.

**TIM**   Faker.

**EDDIE**   What were you doing?

**TIM**   Nothing.

*Eddie turns him over and sits on his chest, grabbing his wrists, and with his knees on his upper arms. He is hurting him.*

**EDDIE**   What were you doing on that rock?

**TIM**   Nothing...

**EDDIE**   If you don't tell me, I'll hit you, and if you tell me a lie, I'll know and hit you twice as hard.

**TIM**   I was signalling to my dad – you can see my garden from here– *(Eddie slaps him.)* I was flying.

**EDDIE**   You what?

**TIM**   You heard.

**EDDIE**    Alright then, show me. *(He climbs off Tim and lets him get up.)* I want to see you fly. *(He pushes Tim towards the rock.)*

**TIM**      I can't do it when someone's watching.

**EDDIE**    Course you can't.

*Pause.*

**TIM**      Can I have my book back?

**EDDIE**    Maybe.

**TIM**      Can I have it now?

**EDDIE**    No. *(Pause)* Why'd you come up here? No-one comes up here.

**TIM**      Somewhere to go. *(Pause)* Miss Adams made me do a project in juniors, I came up here for that.

**EDDIE**    What project?

**TIM**      Caradoc and the Romans. It's all in that book you nicked off us, she gave it me, and I've got to give it back...

**EDDIE**    Alright, alright... So you come up here because of this project thing?

**TIM**      Not any more, I finished it. This is where he fought his last battle.

**EDDIE**    Is it?

**TIM**      If you'd bothered to read my book, you'd know it was.

**EDDIE**    What happened then? In this battle?

**TIM**      He ambushed the Romans, but there were too many of em, so he escaped, and went to this other king for protection, but this king was traitor, and betrayed him to the Romans.

*Pause.*

**EDDIE**    Come here.

| | |
|---|---|
| **TIM** | What for? |
| **EDDIE** | Come here. *(Tim gets up.)* Hit me. |
| **TIM** | No. |
| **EDDIE** | I won't hit you back. |
| **TIM** | I don't want to. |
| **EDDIE** | Try and hit me. |
| **TIM** | Get lost. If you're going to beat me up, just do it. |
| **EDDIE** | I'm not going to beat you up. I want to show you something. But you got to try and hit me first. *(Tim aims a weak slow motion punch at Eddie.)* Properly. *(Tim throws a punch as hard as he can. Eddie twists him round so that his own momentum throws him to the floor, but instead of letting him crash down he catches him.)* My dad showed us that. Now get lost. Go on. *(Tim turns to go.)* And it wasn't some king who betrayed him, it was a woman, Cartimunda, the queen of the Brigantes. |

*Tim exits. Eddie waits until he has gone and then climbs on the rock tries to fly. It doesn't work and he jumps off the rock.*

*A school bell rings. Miss enters.*

## 7.

*At school – a typical UK comprehensive.*

| | |
|---|---|
| **MISS** | Eddie! |
| **EDDIE** | Yes, Miss? |
| **MISS** | You weren't in registration. |
| **EDDIE** | I had to see Mr Brooks, but he wasn't there, Miss. |
| **MISS** | You in trouble again? |
| **EDDIE** | Don't think so, Miss. |

| | |
|---|---|
| **MISS** | Be careful, Eddie. I persuaded him to give you another chance last term, I won't be able to do it a second time. You've been missing lessons. |
| **EDDIE** | I've been to school every single day, Miss. |
| **MISS** | Did I say you hadn't? |
| **EDDIE** | No, Miss. |
| **MISS** | Well? |
| **EDDIE** | I wa'n't very well, Miss, but I thought if I stopped off I'd be in bother. |
| **MISS** | What's been the matter with you? |
| **EDDIE** | Stomach, Miss. |
| **MISS** | Really. So where were you for... *(She consults a list.)* Geography last Wednesday, French on Tuesday, and last Friday, PE once this week and twice the week before? |
| **EDDIE** | In the toilet, Miss. |
| **MISS** | How awful for you. Is it all cleared up now? |
| **EDDIE** | Yes, Miss. |
| **MISS** | It'd better be. Somewhere in there, Eddie, you've got a brain. I don't care if you don't use it, but, you will, one day, if you mess it all up. Let me down if you want to, I'll be sorry, for a few minutes, then I'll get on with my job and forget all about you. But don't you dare let yourself down. Are you listening to me? |
| **EDDIE** | Yes, Miss. |
| **MISS** | Well then? |
| **EDDIE** | I won't, Miss, I promise. |
| **MISS** | Why do I keep on believing you? |
| **EDDIE** | Don't know, Miss, nobody else does. |
| **MISS** | I must be mad. Go on, off you go. Don't want to be late for PE, do you? |

# 8.

*At Eddie's house. Ron is playing his guitar, through a practice amp. He's the ultimate guitar hero. Eddie enters, grimaces, and tries to speak to Ron, but can't make himself heard. Ron has to stop playing.*

**RON**　　What?

**EDDIE**　D'you see your mate?

**RON**　　What mate?

**EDDIE**　The one you said could get us that Man U strip.

**RON**　　Oh, him. Yeah. He han't got none left.

**EDDIE**　Right.

**RON**　　He'll be getting some more.

**EDDIE**　Whatever.

*Ron is about to start playing again, then he remembers.*

**RON**　　Hold on a minute. What's this?

**EDDIE**　A letter.

**RON**　　Don't be clever. D'you know who it's from?

**EDDIE**　No.

**RON**　　Your Mr Brooks. '...we request your full co-operation in making sure that Edward complies with all the above points, his continued presence at this school depends upon an immediate change of attitude.'

**EDDIE**　It's not me, it's them.

**RON**　　Sounds like you've got right up his nose. *(Eddie shrugs.)* No kit, detentions, no homework, you're late, playing truant... If you don't go to school, where do you go?

**EDDIE**　Nowhere.

**RON**　　Why don't you go to school?

| | |
|---|---|
| **EDDIE** | You never. I go to history. |
| **RON** | Maths, English, science, that's what you need. |
| **EDDIE** | They're always on at me. Making out I'm thick. |
| **RON** | He doesn't think you are. Ah, well, you do what you like. |
| **EDDIE** | Is that it? |
| **RON** | It's your life, I can't stop you doing what you want with it. |
| **EDDIE** | Mum would have given me a real bollocking. |

*Ron gives Eddie the letter.*

| | |
|---|---|
| **RON** | Then she'd better have this, hadn't she? Why don't you give it to her next time you see her. *(Eddie wants to respond, but Ron has started to play again. Eddie exits.)* |

## 9.

*Tim comes home from school. He is a hurry to go out, but Mum intercepts him.*

| | |
|---|---|
| **MUM** | Hello, love, good day? |
| **TIM** | Yeah. |
| **MUM** | Cup of tea? |
| **TIM** | No, it's alright. *(Tim dumps his bag and disappears to his room.)* |
| **MUM** | I'm making one for me. |
| **TIM** | No thanks. |

*Mum picks up Tim's bag and feels the weight.*

| | |
|---|---|
| **MUM** | Have they given you lots of homework? |

*Tim reappears ready to go out.*

| | |
|---|---|
| **TIM** | No. *(He takes the bag from Mum and puts it down.)* |

| | |
|---|---|
| **MUM** | Have you got any homework? |
| **TIM** | Yeah. |
| **MUM** | But you're going out? |
| **TIM** | Yeah. I'm going to do it later. |
| **MUM** | It's alright, I trust you organise your own time. Going anywhere in particular? |
| **TIM** | Just out. |
| **MUM** | Just out. |
| **TIM** | Yeah. *(Pause)* You alright? |
| **MUM** | Me? Why shouldn't I be? |
| **TIM** | I don't know. |
| **MUM** | I'm fine. Made any new friends? |
| **TIM** | Yeah, some. |
| **MUM** | Who? |
| **TIM** | Just kids. |
| **MUM** | Well, that's good, isn't it? |

*Pause.*

| | |
|---|---|
| **TIM** | Do you want me to do something? |
| **MUM** | No. |
| **TIM** | Then can I go please? |

*Mum stands back to let him pass.*


## 10.


*After school.*

*Tim enters. Eddie enters.*

| | |
|---|---|
| EDDIE | It's the birdboy. |
| TIM | Hello, Faker. *(Pause)* You weren't on the bus today. Or yesterday. You been sick? |
| EDDIE | What's it to you? *(Pause)* I've been helping me dad. |
| TIM | What doing? Only asking. |
| EDDIE | He's turning the back room into a recording studio. |
| TIM | What for? |
| EDDIE | So he can make his own demos. |
| TIM | Cool. I wish my dad did stuff like that. I remembered about him being on *Millionaire* this month. |
| EDDIE | You being funny? |
| TIM | I haven't seen him yet. |
| EDDIE | Yeah, well, he was supposed to be on last week, but he got sick so he had to ring up and say he couldn't do it. |
| TIM | That's bad. |
| EDDIE | They said they'll let him go in the next series. |
| TIM | My dad watched one. He'd have won £600,000, if he'd been on. |
| EDDIE | Why wasn't he then? |
| TIM | He said it costs a fortune in telephone calls just to get through the preliminary questions. |
| EDDIE | My dad did it on his first call. *(Pause)* You still here? |
| TIM | You going up the Knoll again? |
| EDDIE | What for? |
| TIM | Dunno. |
| EDDIE | No, and neither are you. *(Pause)* Why you always hanging around? |
| TIM | I'm not. |

**EDDIE**     You think I'm your mate or something?

**TIM**       No.

**EDDIE**     Stay off the Knoll, and keep away from me. Got it?

**TIM**       I've got just as much right to be there as you have.

*Eddie grabs his arm and twists it up behind his back.*

**EDDIE**     Yeah? Have yer? You sure? *(Eddie pushes him away.)*

**TIM**       And I want my book back.

**EDDIE**     Get stretched.

*Eddie exits. Tim is left alone for a moment before he leaves in the opposite direction.*

## 11.

*Tim's Mum enters. She has a phone with her. She dials a number as Tim's Dad enters.*

**MUM**       I was just about to ring you.

**DAD**       Something wrong?

**MUM**       Wondering where you were that's all.

**DAD**       Well, now you know where I am, I'm here. *(He kisses her briefly.)* Where's Tim?

**MUM**       Out.

**DAD**       Did he tell you where he was going?

**MUM**       What do you think?

**DAD**       Can't give a straight answer to simple question, that boy. I am shattered.

**MUM**       Where've you been?

**DAD**       When?

| | |
|---|---|
| **MUM** | Today, this evening. |
| **DAD** | At work. And coming home. In that order. |
| **MUM** | You're later then you usually are. |
| **DAD** | I know, tell me about it. |

*Tim arrives unseen by his parents.*

| | |
|---|---|
| **MUM** | Do you really have to do all this extra work? |
| **DAD** | Yes, I do. Because I've got someone on my back about sending our son to a private school. Anna, you know what it's like. There's a lot of pressure on, this time of the year. |
| **MUM** | Are you still going to Zurich next week? I'm only asking, so I know where I stand. |
| **DAD** | Yes, I am going to Zurich next week. |
| **MUM** | Can't you send anyone else to stand in for you? |
| **DAD** | Of course, I can't. *(Pause)* This is all in your imagination, you know. |
| **MUM** | Is it? |
| **DAD** | Yes. |
| **TIM** | Can I have my tea now? |
| **DAD** | Hello, son, had a good day? |
| **TIM** | Yes, thanks. |
| **DAD** | Great. Been out, mum says. |
| **TIM** | Yes. |
| **DAD** | With your mates? |
| **TIM** | Sort of. |
| **DAD** | Not round someone's house? Not playing on the rec? Just out? Yeah? |
| **TIM** | Yeah. |
| **DAD** | Got anything particular in for tea? |

| | |
|---|---|
| **MUM** | I was waiting for you both to come home to see what you wanted. |
| **DAD** | Well, I tell you what. Why don't I nip out and get us a pizza? Then you won't have to do any cooking and we can all have a doss in front of the telly. |
| **MUM** | You're going out again? |
| **DAD** | To get a pizza. |
| **MUM** | You've only just got in. |
| **DAD** | Does it matter? |
| **MUM** | It'll be quicker if I stick something in the microwave. |
| **DAD** | You fancy a pizza, Tim? |
| **TIM** | Yeah. |
| **DAD** | Right. Decision made. Come on then, don't just stand there, I need you to help me choose the toppings. See you later, love. *(Tim and his Dad exit.)* |

## 12.

*On the Knoll.*

*Eddie is on the Knoll. Tim arrives with a bag.*

| | |
|---|---|
| **TIM** | You want the Knoll, fight me for it. |
| **EDDIE** | You? Want to fight me? |
| **TIM** | Yeah. *(Tim pulls two swords out of the bag and throws them on the ground.)* Winner has the Knoll. |

*Eddie picks up the swords.*

| | |
|---|---|
| **EDDIE** | You're on. *(Eddie hands one to Tim. They are uncertain how to begin. Tim bows. So does Eddie. Tim adopts a fencing stance and Eddie knocks the sword straight out of his hand. Tim scrabbles for the sword, gripping it* |

*with both hands. He parries Eddie's blows. Tim attempts an attack himself, and slips, dropping his sword. Eddie stands over him, and then steps back, lets him pick it up. Eddie overpowers Tim. They have both enjoyed the fight. Eddie holds his sword to Tim's throat. Tim kneels. Eddie lifts Tim's head with the tip of his sword.)* Do you know who I am?

**TIM**      You are Caradoc, king of the Catuvellauni.

**EDDIE**    Who are you?

**TIM**      I live in the village, sire.

**EDDIE**    You know why I have come here?

**TIM**      To defeat the Romans.

**EDDIE**    Aren't you frightened?

**TIM**      I'm trying not to be.

**EDDIE**    You could be safe in your bed, and yet you choose to come and join us. Pick up your sword, when next you lay it down, it will be red with Roman blood.

*Tim picks up his sword. Eddie looks out across the valley.*

**TIM**      When will they come, sire?

**EDDIE**    My spies say they'll be here by midday tomorrow. And we'll be waiting for them. You see that ridge of rocks above the river?

**TIM**      Yes, your Majesty.

**EDDIE**    And below, the line of trees? That's where we'll hide our archers. If any man looses an arrow before the Romans are crossing the river, I swear I'll kill him with my bare hands. Our only chance is to strike when they are at their weakest.

**TIM**      And what about us, sire, what do the soldiers do?

**EDDIE**    You? You will pour down the side of this hill like a river of death and cut them to pieces.

*Tim picks up the swords and puts them in his bag.*

**TIM**     See you then.

**EDDIE**   Where you going?

**TIM**     You won.

**EDDIE**   You can stay if you want.

*Pause.*

**TIM**     Why'd he lose? When he'd got it all planned. Maybe there were more of them than he thought. Maybe he ran out of arrows.

**EDDIE**   The Romans had this thing, right, where they'd all stand together in a group, and the ones in the middle would hold their shields over their heads, and the ones round the edges would face outwards.

**TIM**     Like a big tortoise.

**EDDIE**   That's it. So you could chuck anything at them and it'd bounce off.

**TIM**     Burning arrows'd do it.

**EDDIE**   Probably didn't have any. Probably thought the smoke from the fires would give them away.

**TIM**     Dead bad, see that coming at you.

*Tim looses off arrows down the hill, making the sounds as he does so.*

**EDDIE**   Hold your fire until you are sure of your target.

**TIM**     It's no use, sire, we can't hold them back, our arrows are no use, they're bouncing off the shields.

*Eddie picks up a sword from the bag.*

**EDDIE**   In that case we fight them where we stand. Swords at the ready! Wait for my command. Prepare yourselves... *(Eddie steps down. Relaxes.)*

**TIM**     Everything in the whole world would've been different if they'd have won.

*Eddie holds the sword to Tim's throat. Tim is unsure if they are still playing or not.*

**EDDIE**    Can you be trusted?

**TIM**     Course.

*Eddie steps away from the edge of the hill.*

*He puts the sword back in the bag.*

**EDDIE**    I've got something that proves it happened here. *(Eddie hesitates.)* If you say a word about this, you're dead, right? *(Eddie goes to the rock where Caradoc's sword is hidden and takes it out, lays it on the ground. He slowly unwraps the cloth.)* The blade's real, I fixed the hilt. It's Pre-Roman.

**TIM**     Yeah?

**EDDIE**    I found one on a website looks just like it.

**TIM**     Can I hold it? *(Tim tries a few strokes.)*

**EDDIE**    Give it here. *(Tim hands the sword back.)* Stand there, and don't move. *(Eddie performs the same set of strokes he did at the opening of the play round Tim's head. Tim doesn't move an inch. To finish Eddie raises the sword and brings it down, fast to stop inches above Tim's head.)*

**TIM**     That's fantastic.

**EDDIE**    Now you've seen it, you can't tell anyone. You got to swear that.

**TIM**     I will.

**EDDIE**    I need something of yours. Something special. Something really important. Go home for it if you have to.

*Pause.*

| | |
|---|---|
| **TIM** | You've already got something of mine. |
| **EDDIE** | Yeah, right. *(Eddie goes to where he's thrown down his jacket and takes Tim's book out of his pocket. He gives it to Tim, who holds it and goes to hand it back to Eddie, but Eddie stops him, and invites him to put the book in the cloth with the sword himself. He wraps them up, and replaces the bundle.)* From now on, we trust each other. Agreed? |
| **TIM** | Yes. |
| **EDDIE** | And whatever happens, you and me, we never lie, to each other. |
| **TIM** | And if you need the sword, or I need the book, we can take them out but they mustn't leave the Knoll. |
| **EDDIE** | OK. You swear. |
| **TIM** | I swear. *(Eddie spits on his palm. Tim does the same. Eddie holds out his arm to Tim, bent at the elbow as if for arm wrestling. Tim clasps his hand, and starts to giggle.)* |
| **EDDIE** | Shut up. |
| **TIM** | Sorry. |
| **EDDIE** | If we're in trouble, this is the place we come. |
| **TIM** | If one of us needs help, all he has to do is ask. |
| **EDDIE** | Till death. |
| **TIM** | Till death. |

*Pause.*

| | |
|---|---|
| **EDDIE** | Don't laugh. |
| **TIM** | I'm not. |
| **EDDIE** | Don't laugh, I said. |
| **TIM** | You are. |

**EDDIE**   Yeah? *(Eddie holds his face as straight as possible.)*

**TIM**   Alright, you're not.

**EDDIE**   D'you want to see something else I've got?

**TIM**   Alright, yeah. *(Eddie reveals the entrance to his hide-out. It's amazing.)* It's brilliant. *(They squeeze inside.)*

**EDDIE**   Found it by accident. I was jumping about on the rocks, and fell in, head first.

**TIM**   It's fantastic. You could be up here forever and nobody would know you were here. Do you think it was part of the fort?

**EDDIE**   Could be. It's where I found the sword.

**TIM**   I bet he used it. He must have done. I bet he'd have his generals in here, planning it all. Caradoc's Cave. I bet he slept in here too. You ever slept in here?

**EDDIE**   Yeah, loads of times. I spent a whole week up here once... No, I didn't, thought about it though.

**TIM**   It'd be great to camp out up here. *(Tim is fascinated. He keeps picking things up, mugs, pieces of wood, a kitchen knife, candles, comics.)*

**TIM**   Does anybody else know about this place?

**EDDIE**   No.

**TIM**   Not even your dad?

**EDDIE**   I wouldn't tell him anything I din't want the whole village to know.

**TIM**   I won't tell nobody.

**EDDIE**   I know.

**TIM**   Can't we keep the sword and the book in here? Stop the book getting all damp, won't it? And you'd have the sword right next to you if anyone attacked.

**EDDIE**   Alright. *(Tim goes and gets the bundle, passes it to Eddie. Eddie arranges the cloth, the sword and book in the den.)* Right. Come on, I'll show you how to close it.

**TIM**   Can't we stay here for a bit?

**EDDIE**   I've got things to do. *(Eddie closes it up.)* Do it like this, and nobody'll ever find it. You can use it on your own if you want...

**TIM**   I won't.

**EDDIE**   You might as well.

*Pause.*

**TIM**   If I do, I'll be really careful.

**EDDIE**   You'd better be. Or...

**TIM**   I know – I'm dead. *(Pause)* Why d'you show me all this?

**EDDIE**   Cos I did. But it don't mean I want you hanging around me down there.

**TIM**   I won't.

**EDDIE**   Keep out of my way, then I won't have to do nothing. You can always text me though.

**TIM**   My mum won't let me have a phone, she says it'll only get nicked.

**EDDIE**   Then we'll make out that I've made you do my homework, then you've got an excuse to pass me anything you like.

**TIM**   Yeah. Alright. But I'm not though, am I?

**EDDIE**   Are you stupid? No, you're not. *(They start to go down the hill.)* Not together. Give me a few minutes, then go down by the plantation.

**TIM**   OK. *(Eddie sets off.)* Faker?

**EDDIE**   Yeah?

| | |
|---|---|
| **TIM** | It's the best thing I've ever seen. *(Eddie exits. Tim climbs on to the rock and looks out over the village. He waits, checks his watch, then exits.)* |

## 13.

*Ron fetches on stage a guitar case, a practice amp, and his bag. Eddie enters.*

| | |
|---|---|
| **EDDIE** | What's all this? |
| **RON** | I've got a job. |
| **EDDIE** | What doing? |
| **RON** | There's this band... |
| **EDDIE** | Oh, yeah? |
| **RON** | They're thrash metal, but I don't mind. |
| **EDDIE** | They want you to play? |
| **RON** | Not exactly play. They want me to drive the van. |
| **EDDIE** | What's the guitar for then? |
| **RON** | You never know, do you? Right, I'm off. |
| **EDDIE** | When you back? |
| **RON** | Ten days, tops. |
| **EDDIE** | You what? |
| **RON** | I'm going back on the road. |
| **EDDIE** | You're leaving me on me own? |
| **RON** | Well, I can't take you with me, can I? Come on... I'd have killed for a chance to be left on me own when I was your age. |
| **EDDIE** | What am I supposed to do? |

| | |
|---|---|
| **RON** | There's more than enough money, in the kitchen, behind the clock. You'll be fine. |
| | It means I trust you, dun'it? I respect your ability to function in the world as an independent person. I couldn't go, if I didn't. |
| **EDDIE** | You can't go. |
| **RON** | I'll be back before you miss me. |
| **EDDIE** | You're not allowed to, I'm not old enough to live on me own. What happens if someone finds out? |
| **RON** | You keep your mouth shut, and they won't. Look after yourself, and don't trash the place. |
| **EDDIE** | Dad, you can't. |
| **RON** | If you don't like it, go and stay with your mother. *(Ron exits.)* |
| **EDDIE** | Dad... |

*Music. Eddie exits.*

## 14.

*Tim's mother enters.*

| | |
|---|---|
| **MUM** | What have you got there? |
| **TIM** | Just stuff. |
| **MUM** | Let me see. *(She pulls the swords out of his bag.)* |
| **MUM** | You made these? |
| **TIM** | For school. |
| **MUM** | They're very good. You're not really happy here, are you? |
| **TIM** | Yes, I am. |
| **MUM** | You hate the comp. |

| | |
|---|---|
| **TIM** | No, I don't. |
| **MUM** | What if we moved? |
| **TIM** | Now? |
| **MUM** | Yes, now. Wouldn't you like that? New school, new place to live. A fresh start. It's the right time to do it, you're only just half way through your first term. |
| **TIM** | Is dad being moved to a new job? |
| **MUM** | What's it got to do with your father? |
| **TIM** | Well, you know... moving? |
| **MUM** | It's something I've been thinking about. |
| **TIM** | What does dad say though? |
| **MUM** | If you see him, why don't you ask him? |
| **TIM** | So we're not really moving then? |
| **MUM** | We might be. It's something for you to think about. |
| **TIM** | Are you alright? |
| **MUM** | Yes, I'm fine. |
| **TIM** | Mum, can I camp out? |
| **MUM** | What? |
| **TIM** | Camp out. In a tent. |
| **MUM** | Where? |
| **TIM** | In the garden. Can I? |
| **MUM** | I suppose so. |
| **TIM** | Cool. |
| **MUM** | It'll be very cold. Why don't you wait till summer? |
| **TIM** | No, I want to do it now. |
| **MUM** | Alright, you can do it now. *(Tim goes to leave.)* Where you going, you've only just got in? |

| TIM | I'm going up to my room. I've got homework. |
|-----|-----|
| **MUM** | Yes, of course, sorry… |
| **TIM** | Get a grip, Mum, eh? *(Tim exits.)* |

## 15.

*On The Knoll. Eddie approaches the den. He looks around him and whistles and the den opens. Tim is inside. He has brought all sorts of stuff from home. There are bowls, cutlery, plates, and mugs. He's sitting in front of a GAZ stove heating soup. The den's lit by candles.*

| **TIM** | I thought you weren't coming. |
|-----|-----|
| **EDDIE** | Very good. *(Eddie picks up a tin.)* Asparagus Tips? |
| **TIM** | They're alright, but they make your wee smell like rubber. |
| **EDDIE** | No thanks. *(Eddie picks up a telescope.)* |
| **TIM** | I've brought some binoculars as well. Want some soup? *(Tim gives Eddie some soup. Eddie wolfs it down.)* |
| **EDDIE** | D'you want any more of this? |
| **TIM** | I've had some. *(Eddie takes the pan and finishes the lot. He looks round the den.)* |
| **EDDIE** | Where'd it all come from? |
| **TIM** | Out of our garage. |
| **EDDIE** | It's better'n most the stuff we got in our house. An iPhone… |
| **TIM** | My dad gave it me, you can have it, I don't want it. |
| **EDDIE** | Yeah. They'll say I nicked it. |
| **TIM** | Say you borrowed it. |
| **EDDIE** | Off you? How we going to clean all this stuff? Leave it lying around we'll get ants. |

**TIM**   I brought some bottles of water up from the river, I fetched these from home. *(He produces washing up liquid, a scourer, a small bowl, and a tea towel.)*

**EDDIE**   I don't believe you! *(They wash up, then put the things away, and Tim goes out of the tent and sits on a rock. Eddie joins him.)*

**TIM**   Do you ever look at a star and wonder if someone's up there, looking back at you?

**EDDIE**   No, cos I'm not soft in the head.

*Pause.*

**EDDIE**   Will your mum and dad check up on you?

**TIM**   I didn't go till their light went out. Dad's alarm's 6.30, I've set mine for six, that's loads of time. You alright?

**EDDIE**   No problem.

**TIM**   Heavy sleeper, your dad?

**EDDIE**   He's not there. He's off driving for this band. Ten days, he said.

**TIM**   You've got the place to yourself for ten days?

**EDDIE**   Yeah.

**TIM**   Hey, that's great. You can do what you like, go to bed when you like, eat what you like. God, I wish I could get rid of my mum and dad for ten days. Ten minutes would be good. These kids saying they reckoned you were home alone.

**EDDIE**   Oh, great.

**TIM**   I'll say they're lying, say I saw your dad, or something.

*Pause.*

**EDDIE**   Three weeks ago he went. He hasn't even bloody phoned... You know they call me Faker? Started when I was little. I used to believe everything my dad said. Like, we're going to Eurodisney for me birthday, and I'd tell everybody. Said he was going to take me on one of them tours round Man U's ground. Never happened. He promised loads of stuff like that. Never even took me to the pictures. He tells lies all the time, and I tell more lies to cover up for him.

**TIM**      Your dad doesn't tell actual lies...

**EDDIE**   So he is really going to be on *Millionaire* then? And he did give David Beckham a lift when his car broke down and got invited back to meet Victoria?

**TIM**      Everybody makes up stories, pretending.

**EDDIE**   You pretend you can fly, but you don't try to make the whole village believe you can really do it. He makes me sick.

**TIM**      My mum thinks my dad is having an affair. She's always on the phone crying to my Auntie Pat about it.

**EDDIE**   Is he?

**TIM**      Don't think so. He spends all his time at work. It's the only way he can get away from my mum going at him. Now she's on about moving.

**EDDIE**   Yeah.

**TIM**      It won't happen. It's all in her head.

*Pause.*

**TIM**      Come on. *(Tim climbs on his rock and stretches his arms out.)*

**EDDIE**   I can't do this.

**TIM**      Course you can. *(Eddie gets up on a rock. He copies Tim.)*

**TIM**      Ready? One... two... three...! *(Both boys take to the air. Aware of each other, relaxed and free. They finish flying.)*

**EDDIE**   I wish I could do that for real.

*Pause.*

**TIM**     Why don't you go and stop with your mum?

**EDDIE**   She lives in Birmingham.

**TIM**     It's not that far. My mum went to gran's once and took me with her. I had nearly three weeks off school with everyone making a fuss of me in case we turned into a single parent family.

**EDDIE**   My mum took me with her when she left.

**TIM**     Did you ask to go back to your dad then?

**EDDIE**   Did I hell. She sent me back. She's living with this bloke, Clive. He's got two daughters, and they were supposed to share, and I'm supposed to have my own room, but all I got was a mattress on the landing. She said I'd have to stay with me dad until they got a bigger place.

**TIM**     And they haven't?

*Pause.*

**TIM**     D'you want to sleep out, or go back inside?

**EDDIE**   Inside, yeah? *(They go back inside the den and close it behind them. Pause.)*

**EDDIE**   D'you want it open or closed?

**TIM**     Don't mind.

**EDDIE**   Closed then. *(Together they start to close up the den.)*

## 16.

*Ron comes home before Eddie gets back from the cave. Eddie enters but he doesn't see Ron.*

**RON**     Where the hell have you been?

**EDDIE**   When did you get back?

**RON**    You weren't here.

**EDDIE**    You said you'd only be ten days.

**RON**    Don't change the subject. Where've you been?

**EDDIE**    Get lost.

**RON**    I want a straight answer. And don't give me none of your lies. I want to know where you bin. *(Eddie doesn't reply.)* Three o'clock this morning I got back. I went into your room, see if you're alright. No sign of you.

**EDDIE**    I was camping out.

**RON**    On your own?

**EDDIE**    Yeah.

**RON**    D'you tell anyone I've been working away?

**EDDIE**    No.

**RON**    You better not. Have you been missing school?

**EDDIE**    No.

**RON**    That's alright then.

*Pause.*

**RON**    Place looks OK. Better 'an when I left. Look, I didn't want to come back here and go off on one, but I was worried, alright? I thought something might have happened to you.

**EDDIE**    Well, it hasn't.

**RON**    Yeah. Alright. Hang on, I've got something for you. *(Ron goes out and comes back in with a large cardboard box.)*

**EDDIE**    What is it?

**RON**    Open it and see. *(Eddie opens the box. He takes out a black T-shirt.)*

**EDDIE**    There's loads of them. *(He holds the T-shirt out. It has IRON LUNG and a logo printed on it.)* Iron Lung.

| | |
|---|---|
| **RON** | They couldn't sell 'em all, so I brought these back for you. Here. *(Ron roots about in the box, and takes out a T-shirt in a polythene bag.)* I got the lads to sign this one specially for you. That makes it a collectors item. *(Eddie puts the T-shirt back in the box.)* Keep you going for a bit, won't they? |
| **EDDIE** | Yeah. Thanks a lot. |
| **RON** | I've got a CD an' all. Hey, Dazza, he's lead guitar, one night right, he split his finger end halfway through the second number and I stood in for him while he went off and found a plaster. It was three and a half songs before he was back. Where you going? |
| **EDDIE** | To have a bath. |
| **RON** | Yeah, course. You done alright, you know that? Looking after yourself, and this place. *(Eddie exits with the box.)* Hey! |
| **EDDIE** | What? |
| **RON** | Anything in the fridge? |

### 17.

*At Tim's house. Dad enters.*

| | |
|---|---|
| **MUM** | Do they know any more? |
| **DAD** | They're starting a search. Everyone's to check their outbuildings. |
| **MUM** | Is there anything we can do? |
| **DAD** | Let the police to get on with it. |
| **MUM** | Do they think he's been... abducted? |
| **DAD** | They're not saying. |

| | |
|---|---|
| **MUM** | He doesn't seem the type. He wouldn't let somebody grab him, he'd put up a fight. |
| **DAD** | His idiot of a father left him in that house all on his own for nearly a month, while he's off driving a van for some rock band. Can you believe it? Some people shouldn't be allowed to have kids. |
| **MUM** | You don't think...? |
| **DAD** | His father? No. |
| **MUM** | What's the time? |
| **DAD** | About five. |
| **MUM** | He should be back by now. He wasn't on the school bus. |
| **DAD** | He's probably got a football practice. |
| **MUM** | Tim doesn't play football. |
| **DAD** | Well, there'll be something. |
| **MUM** | Yes, of course. |
| **DAD** | He won't be long. |
| **MUM** | You're not going back to work tonight, are you? |
| **DAD** | No, love. |

## 18.

*On the Knoll.*

*Tim approaches the den cautiously.*

*He has the school bag with him.*

| | |
|---|---|
| **TIM** | Faker? Faker? Eddie? *(The den opens and Eddie comes out.)* I knew you'd be here. I've come straight up from the bus. |
| **EDDIE** | Anyone see you? |

| | |
|---|---|
| **TIM** | No. I made sure. |
| **EDDIE** | Go on then, what's been happening? |
| **TIM** | There's police everywhere, we had a special assembly and anyone who thought they knew anything about where you were... |
| **EDDIE** | You didn't say? |
| **TIM** | Don't be stupid, course I didn't. I saw your dad. |
| **EDDIE** | He was there when I got back. *(Pause)* I can't even stand being in the same room with him any more. |
| **TIM** | Is that why you're up here? He didn't hit you, did he? |
| **EDDIE** | He wouldn't dare. |
| **TIM** | Did you have a big row and walk out, or something? |
| **EDDIE** | Better than that. I cooked him his tea, listened to his poxy CD, went to bed, got up, made breakfast, left the house as if I was going to school, then when he'd gone out, went back, got me stuff, and came here. |
| **TIM** | Cool. So how long are you going stay up here? |
| **EDDIE** | As long as it takes. |
| **TIM** | Takes for what? |
| **EDDIE** | For me to get what I want. |
| **TIM** | Yeah. Right. |
| **EDDIE** | And you've got to help me. I've got enough for now, but I'm going to need more food and stuff, and someone to tell me what's going on. |
| **TIM** | I'll do that, no problem. |
| **EDDIE** | If you let on I'm up here, or someone sees you... |
| **TIM** | They won't, I'll make sure. |
| **EDDIE** | Come on. I've made a list. *(They go inside the den.)* |

## 19.

*At Tim's house.*

**MUM**   It is getting late now.

**DAD**   He'll be here soon. *(Tim enters.)* What did I tell you? Where've you been?

**TIM**   Coming home from school.

**MUM**   You weren't on the school bus.

**TIM**   I know.

**DAD**   So where were you?

**TIM**   I was on the regular bus.

**MUM**   Why were you on the regular bus?

**TIM**   Because I stayed at school.

**DAD**   Dear God...

**TIM**   I stayed behind, and it wasn't because I was kept in, it was cos I was half way through this experiment and it went all wrong so she let me do it again.

**MUM**   Your teacher?

**TIM**   Yes.

**DAD**   And that's why you're late?

**TIM**   Yes.

**MUM**   You know a boy from the village has gone missing.

**TIM**   They had a special assembly to tell us about it.

**DAD**   Do you know him?

**TIM**   He's not in my year. *(Tim exits.)*

**DAD**   He's home.

**MUM**   But if it had been him.

| | |
|---|---|
| **DAD** | That's enough. *(Tim enters ready to go out.)* |
| **TIM** | I'm off out, alright? |
| **DAD** | No, it's not alright. |
| **TIM** | What? |
| **DAD** | Your mother wants you to stay in. |
| **TIM** | Why? |
| **MUM** | I would have thought it was obvious. |
| **TIM** | Nothing's going to happen to me, there's loads of police about. |
| **DAD** | You're staying in. |
| **TIM** | I don't want to. |
| **MUM** | Not tonight, Tim. |
| **TIM** | I always go out. |
| **DAD** | Did you hear what we said? |
| **TIM** | I can't do anything in this place. *(Tim stomps off.)* |
| **DAD** | God help us when he's a teenager. You OK to hold the fort for a bit? |
| **MUM** | But you said... |
| **DAD** | Half an hour – tops. |

## 20.

*On the Knoll. Tim is looking around for Eddie.*

*Eddie leaps out, he has Caradoc's sword in his hand. He holds the point to Tim's chest.*

| | |
|---|---|
| **TIM** | Hey! Leave off! |
| **EDDIE** | Were you followed? |

| | |
|---|---|
| **TIM** | No. |
| **EDDIE** | No, my liege. |
| **TIM** | No, my liege. |
| **EDDIE** | Have you spoken of where I am? |
| **TIM** | Course I haven't. *(Eddie jabs him with the sword.)* There are spies in the village, who seek to know of your whereabouts, but they will learn nothing from me, sire. |
| **EDDIE** | Was I right to place my trust in you? |
| **TIM** | Yes, your Majesty. *(Eddie lowers the sword.)* |
| **EDDIE** | What are you carrying in your sack? |
| **TIM** | Two tins of beans and a packet of penguins. |
| **EDDIE** | Brilliant. |
| **TIM** | I had to take it all to school with me. *(Eddie attacks the bag.)* |
| **EDDIE** | I had them asparagus tips, you're right, when I had a piss, my wee didn't half stink. |
| **TIM** | I've brought my sleeping bag, thought you'd need two, cos there's snow on the way. |
| **EDDIE** | Great, I was freezing last night. Where you bin? |
| **TIM** | I got grounded. |
| **EDDIE** | What for? |
| **TIM** | It was your fault. |
| **EDDIE** | What'd I do? |
| **TIM** | My stupid mother won't let me out of her sight in case I get 'abducted'. |
| **EDDIE** | They think that's what happened? |
| **TIM** | She does. *(Eddie goes back to the bag.)* |
| **EDDIE** | Carrots? |

| | |
|---|---|
| **TIM** | You've got to have a proper diet, or you'll get ill. |
| **EDDIE** | Yeah... |
| **TIM** | I saw your dad being taken away for questioning. |
| **EDDIE** | Good. |
| **TIM** | You sure you can stay up here like this? It's too cold. You'll need blankets, and food. |
| **EDDIE** | You said you'd help me. |
| **TIM** | I will. |
| **EDDIE** | This in't a game, Tim. |

*Pause.*

| | |
|---|---|
| **TIM** | Is your mum called Julie? |
| **EDDIE** | Yeah. |
| **TIM** | She's down there. |
| **EDDIE** | Has she said anything about me? |
| **TIM** | I dunno. |
| **EDDIE** | I'm not going down just cos she's turned up, it'd be like last time. If they want me, they'll have to come and find me. |
| **TIM** | If they know where to look. |
| **EDDIE** | Help me get this stuff inside. *(Eddie opens the den and Tim helps him take in the stuff he's brought up, and they close the door behind them.)* |

**21.**

*Ron and Julie.*

*Ron enters.*

**RON**　　Julie? *(Julie enters.)*

**JULIE**　What they say?

**RON**　　Nothing new.

**JULIE**　They don't think that you...

**RON**　　Do you?

**JULIE**　Of course, I don't.

**RON**　　Well that's something.

**JULIE**　That was really stupid what you did. A thirteen year old boy.

**RON**　　He's fourteen. Nearly fourteen. I'd have loved it, being on me own at his age. I've got to earn a living. Yeah, well, no, it might not have been too clever, but just cos I give him a bit of freedom, it don't mean I want him to come to any harm...

　　　　　　Does it?

**JULIE**　I've rung home. He's not at our house. Clive says he'll stay off work in case he turns up.

**RON**　　That's big of him. What makes you think he'll come to you?

**JULIE**　I don't know where he's going to go, do I? Neither of us do.

**RON**　　Us? Is that 'us', you and me, or you and Clive?

**JULIE**　Give it a rest, Ron, please. You want to listen to yourself sometimes. How did you make that court believe I wasn't a fit mother?

**RON**　　I don't know.

**JULIE**　If anything happens to him, I'll never forgive you.

**RON**　　Yeah, well, that makes two of us.

**JULIE**　They're going to have you for neglect.

| | |
|---|---|
| **RON** | If they get him back they can do me for what they like. |
| **JULIE** | Is there anywhere, anywhere at all, he might have gone, that we haven't thought of? |
| **RON** | The only place he ever talked of round here was the Knoll. |
| **JULIE** | They went all over it last night, there was no sign of him. |
| **RON** | Then I've no idea. We will get him back, won't we? *(Pause)* I never told him what I done. About making out you were unfit, an' that. And I've never said a word against you, ever. |
| **JULIE** | They want us to go on television. |

## 22.

*On the Knoll.*

*The door of the den opens. Tim comes out, dressed for colder weather. Eddie follows him, wearing clothes Tim has brought.*

| | |
|---|---|
| **TIM** | If the snow lays next time, they'll see my tracks. If that happens I'll put the bag behind our garage. |
| **EDDIE** | If they can see your tracks, they'll see mine too, stupid. |
| **TIM** | OK, I'll leave it in the plantation, then you can get right to the road without anyone seeing you. |
| **EDDIE** | And don't leave it so long next time, you've got to come everyday. |
| **TIM** | You gotta come down. |
| **EDDIE** | No. |
| **TIM** | I'm the only one knows you're up here, it's not fair. What if you get sick? |
| **EDDIE** | I won't get sick. |
| **TIM** | You already sound like you've got flu. |

| | |
|---|---|
| **EDDIE** | I'm fine. |
| **TIM** | What if you freeze to death, what if you get hypothermia and die? It'll be my fault. |
| **EDDIE** | I won't die. |
| **TIM** | I'll be responsible. |
| **EDDIE** | I'll tell everyone I made you do it. |
| **TIM** | You won't be able to tell anybody anything if you're dead. *(Pause)* Why don't you make your escape, sire, while there is still time? |
| **EDDIE** | No. Stand firm with me and all will be well. |
| **TIM** | You've got to come down sometime. |
| **EDDIE** | If they want me, let them come and take me. If they can. |
| **TIM** | But they won't, will they, cos they've already been up here once. |
| **EDDIE** | They'll come. |
| **TIM** | What if I stop bringing you food, you'd have to give up then? |
| **EDDIE** | You wouldn't do that. We promised. *(Eddie climbs on a rock.)* Let's fly. Come on. *(He flexes his legs for take off and raises his arms.)* |
| **TIM** | I've got to go down. *(Tim goes to the cave and picks up the GAZ stove and shakes it.)* You're running out. I'll see if I can get you another. *(Tim exits and Eddie watches him leave, then he goes back into the den and closes it.)* |

## 23.

*It's morning. Ron enters, and starts to play quietly to himself. Simple, basic 12 bar.*

*At Tim's house his mother is waiting for him, time for school.*

*Tim enters. He's not well.*

| | |
|---|---|
| **MUM** | Are you alright? |
| **TIM** | Yeah, I'm fine. |
| **MUM** | Come here. *(She puts her hand on his forehead.)* You've got a temperature. No school for you today. |
| **TIM** | I'm alright. |
| **MUM** | You go to school today, you'll end up spending the next week in bed. |
| **TIM** | But Mum... |
| **MUM** | Upstairs. *(She takes his school bag from him and nearly drops it as the weight takes her by surprise.)* What on earth have you got in here? *(She opens the bag and finds the food he's got to take to Eddie.)* What's all this? |
| **TIM** | We're sending these parcels out to a village in Africa, the whole school's doing it. |
| **MUM** | You surely can't send a GAZ canister? |
| **TIM** | Yeah, you can, cos they pack them all in containers. I told you all about it. |
| **MUM** | Did you? |
| **TIM** | Yes. Look, please let me go. |
| **MUM** | You can take the food in tomorrow. If you're better. |
| **TIM** | Please... |
| **MUM** | Bed. *(Tim exits. Ron finishes playing. Mum clears away Tim's bag.)* |

## 24.

*On the Knoll.*

*The den opens. Eddie looks out. He comes out. It's an effort. He whistles and waits for a reply. He sits and waits. He shivers, stands, takes one last look and goes back into the den. He's about to close it when he hears someone approaching. He pulls the door to look out without being seen. Tim enters. Eddie comes out of the den.*

**EDDIE**  You look terrible.

**TIM**  I've got your flu. Mum's kept me off school, I've got to be back in bed by the time she gets home. Here. *(Eddie takes the bag.)* It's as much as I could get, she found all the stuff in my bag this morning, I had to say it was for a charity thing at school.

**EDDIE**  Don't matter.

**TIM**  Stop doing this. Your picture's all over the place. Last night on the news they said you'd been spotted in Cornwall. Your mum and dad'll be going barmy.

**EDDIE**  Good.

**TIM**  She hasn't gone back to Birmingham. They were on telly the other night, you should have seen them. You got to pack it in.

**EDDIE**  No.

**TIM**  I've had enough.

**EDDIE**  What you say?

**TIM**  I've had enough. And I'm the one who's going to end up getting the blame.

**EDDIE**  You're not coming again, are you? You're not coming again, and you're gonna grass me up.

**TIM**  If you pack it in now, they'll be so pleased you're still alive, you won't get into any bother. They'll listen to you. Why you did it, and everything. I bet you'll end up with your mum, or she'll come back to your dad even. But if you leave it much longer, when they find you, they'll say you're mad, or a danger to yourself or something, and they'll stick you in a home.

EDDIE     Worked it all out, have you?

TIM     Well, you haven't? *(Eddie pulls the sword out of its hiding place and holds it to Tim's throat.)*

EDDIE     Swear you won't betray me!

TIM     You're going to make yourself really ill.

EDDIE     Swear.

TIM     This is stupid.

EDDIE     I said swear. *(The pressure on the sword is starting to hurt Tim.)*

TIM     I swear, OK?

EDDIE     You'd better mean it.

TIM     I mean it. Whatever you want. I don't care any more.

*Pause.*

EDDIE     Are you going to break your promise?

TIM     No. *(Eddie holds the sword above his head and begins to make the same passes that he made before around Tim's head, but they lack the energy of the previous scene. He brings the blade down slowly and lets it rest on Tim's head. Tim takes hold of the blade and takes it off his head.)*

EDDIE     You'd better go before your mum gets back. *(Tim goes into the cave.)* What you doing? *(He comes out with the book.)*

TIM     I've got to take the book back, she only lent it me. She wants it.

EDDIE     You'll come back, won't yer?

TIM     I said, I would din't I? *(Eddie watches him go.)*

**EDDIE**     Have courage and keep safe. You are the most trusted of my followers.

## 25.

*At Tim's house.*

**MUM**     Tim!

*Tim enters.*

**TIM**     Do I have to?

**MUM**     You know how much your gran likes to see you.

**TIM**     I think I've still some got that virus thing, I could infect her.

**MUM**     Of course you won't infect her. After all she's done for you, I think it's really mean if you can't spare her a few hours.

**TIM**     I don't feel well.

**MUM**     There's nothing wrong with you. I can't say I like the way you've been behaving lately, and as far as I'm concerned the sooner you snap out of it the better.

**TIM**     It's started snowing again.

*Dad enters.*

**DAD**     I think the roads'll stay clear. What's up with him?

**MUM**     Nothing. There's a cool box in the kitchen, could you put it in the boot for me.

**DAD**     Yeah, alright. *(Dad exits.)*

**MUM**     Will you go and put your coat on, please? *(Tim doesn't move.)* Tim? What's the matter?

**TIM**     Mum, I think I might have done something really bad, if I tell you, will you get mad at me?

| | |
|---|---|
| **MUM** | How bad? |
| **TIM** | It's not, like a crime, or anything. |
| **MUM** | Is this what's been bothering you? |
| **TIM** | Yeah, sort of. Are you going to be mad? |
| **MUM** | No, course I'm not. *(Pause)* Is it school? |
| **TIM** | No. |

*Dad enters.*

| | |
|---|---|
| **DAD** | I've done that. Oh, come on get a move on, you two... |
| **MUM** | Could you just give us a minute, please? |
| **DAD** | Give you a minute? What for? What's he done now? It'll only be something and nothing. Talk about it in the car, I'm not getting stuck on the ring road again. |
| **TIM** | I want to tell Mum something. |

*Pause.*

| | |
|---|---|
| **DAD** | Fine, go ahead, I'll be in the car. *(Dad exits.)* |
| **MUM** | Go on, Tim. |
| **TIM** | I've been helping somebody do something. |
| **MUM** | And...? |
| **TIM** | It was alright to start with... |
| **MUM** | But not now? |
| **TIM** | Not really. I can't do it any more, it's all going wrong. |
| **MUM** | Does this person know how you feel? |
| **TIM** | I think so. |
| **MUM** | Are they in trouble? |
| **TIM** | They haven't done anything wrong. |
| **MUM** | So we don't need to tell the police? |

**TIM**    No, you can't do that, if he sees the police coming, he'll take off and they'll never find him.

**MUM**    This friend, is it Eddie Mason? Oh, thank God he's safe. You've got to tell his parents, Tim.

**TIM**    He went off cos of his dad.

**MUM**    OK. Where is he?

**TIM**    Faker's on the Knoll, Mum, in this hideout, only me and him know where it is, I'm not supposed to tell cos I promised but it's getting really cold, he'll get sick. I said to come down but he won't, and he wants to wait till they find him, but they won't…

**MUM**    Come on, it's alright, you done the right thing, love. *(Mum fetches Tim's coat.)* Let's you and me go and find your friend.

*Dad enters.*

**DAD**    I've had enough now. It's your mother we're going to see. Where are you two going?

**MUM**    Out.

## 26.

*On the top of the Knoll. Tim and his Mum enter.*

**TIM**    Faker… *(Tim points to the cave.)* He's in there, Mum. *(Tim opens the cave. Mum stops Tim and goes inside. Pause. She comes out. She has a mobile phone in her hand. She's been trying to get a signal.)*

**TIM**    Is he alright?

**MUM**    I can't get a signal.

*Tim tries to go into the cave, but she stops him.*

TIM          I've got to tell him something. *(He breaks away from his mother, and goes into the cave. She gets a signal.)*

MUM          Ambulance please. I'm on top of the Knoll. That's right. There's a boy up here, he's been hiding in a cave. No, I couldn't tell. Listen, it's a really bad signal, we'll come down and meet you and I'll ring you again when we get round to the other side of the hill. Yes, but... Please be as quick as you can.

*The signal goes.*

*Long pause.*

*Tim comes out.*

TIM          He was right down in the sleeping bags. I could only see the top of his head. Was he like that when you went in there?

MUM          Yes.

TIM          I didn't want to wake him.

MUM          The ambulance is on its way, I said I'd ring them again because the signal was so bad. They'll be here soon, we'd better go down and meet them.

TIM          I want to stay here. Let me. Please...

MUM          I'll be as quick as I can.

*Mum exits.*

*Tim goes towards the den. Stops. He climbs onto the rock he uses for flying. He spreads his arms out. Tim starts to soar.*

TIM          Faker...!

*Lights down.*

*The end.*

# MIA

Produced by the Nottingham Playhouse, UK.

First performance at Magnus High School, Newark, 13th October 2004.

Directed by Andrew Breakwell.

## Cast

Mia                          Natalie Wilcox

*A voice is heard in the corridor.*

**MIA**      This one? In here? OK. I will wait in here, and you will go and ask for me? Yes?

*The door opens and Mia comes in, still looking down the corridor. She turns and sees the pupils. She calls down the corridor.*

Excuse me, please! There are some people in this room already.

*She turns back into the room.*

She's gone. Sorry. She said I had to wait. Excuse me.

*She shuts the door.*

How do you get anyone to listen to you in this place? Do you think she understands me? I am speaking English, yes? And pretty well too. I don't speak quietly, I speak very plainly. Now she has gone somewhere to get away from the nasty girl who shouts too much. Perhaps I have frightened her, and she won't come back? No. She will come back.

*She looks at the class.*

You are looking at me.

*She goes and sits on the edge of a desk, preferably a boy's.*

Do I make you nervous?

I would be nervous. Complete stranger. Never seen her before. Bang, bang, bang, right in the middle of the room. Rude too. Doesn't say who she is. No proper introduction.

Too easy to make a boy feel nervous, yes?

Don't worry. You'll be alright.

*Pause.*

She will come back.

*Pause.*

And I will do as I am told and wait here until she does.

Perhaps she will phone for the police? No, if she thought I was a dangerous person then she wouldn't have told me to wait in here with you. I am not a dangerous person. Very good girl, very polite.

OK. Proper introduction. Mia. That's my name. Mia. I should tell you more, I think. Where do I come from? Where have I been?

Everywhere. Too many places. You want me to give them all a name? I can't. You say the name of a place and it's like you are right back there again.

Where is she?

Always this waiting. 'Could you wait, please?' 'Do you mind waiting?' 'I'm afraid you'll have to wait.' I'm very good at waiting. In the last two years I have done so much waiting...for trains, buses, ferries, in police stations, in schools, but not usually in a classroom, nasty girl, don't let her be alone with the nice pupils. In hospitals. And one mortuary. Bad place. In there, I think, I waited forever, but when my waiting came to an end, and I made my legs carry me across that cold white floor, the person I was frightened to see was not the dead one on the trolley. A mortuary is not nice, I tell you. Think very carefully before you go into a place like that, unless, of course, you are dead, and then it doesn't matter because you can't think at all. I think.

*She begins to search through her bag. She puts all her objects on the desk. She finds her mobile phone.*

No messages. No missed calls. And running out of credit.

*She picks up a diary. Inside the pages there is a photograph. She looks at it, rubs it on her sleeve, and puts it back in the diary.*

I was going to be a teacher. I wanted to teach English. Yes. Truly. I had passed all my exams to go to college. Every single one. But... it was not possible. There were a lot of things that were not possible.

I collect things. You've never collect things? Everybody collects things.

*On the desk are an old wallet, some postcards, a belt buckle, a shell, a key, a comb (one handle and long teeth).*

*She picks up a postcard and reads the message.*

'I got here this morning, I'll be home before you get this. Love, Brian'.

Why did he send it, if he's going to be back before the card? Sounds to me like he wanted to prove he'd been there.

*She takes another one.*

'Better for me on the 12th'. What does that mean?

*She puts the postcards away.*

They're not mine. I found all these things. If I see
something that interests me, I pick it up. But I only pick
up what people throw away. See, not a thief, harmless
mad girl.

When I am on a long journey, or I don't know what to do
with myself, I can take something out of my bag, and see
if I can find a story about it. I have to be in the story, of
course, and I try to make it very exciting and glamorous
for me, it's normal.

*She takes out the diary.*

I found this about a year ago on a bench in a park. See, no
name, no address, so I couldn't give it back. It's for 2001
to 2002. There isn't a single entry in it from beginning to
end, so I can put in my own. Let's see. I show you.

March 8th. J.V. Eight o'clock. With three exclamation
marks...

No, that one's private.

Here.

June 14th. Heathrow 0930. New York.

I tell you about that.

My work was going very well, I decided I deserved a small
treat. In this story I earn a lot of money. I love New York.
So I flew out for a week, yes, see, 21st June. JFK 1115.
London. That was my return day, one week later, exactly.
I went on my own. On the plane the seat next to me was
empty right up until the last moment, then this really
smooth, deep voice said, 'Sorry to disturb you, but may I
sit down?' I had left my bag on the seat, you see, so he had
to ask me first. It was this gorgeous man. He sat down,
and after the plane had taken off and we had been served
our first glass of champagne, I only travel on airlines
that give you champagne, we started to talk, and he was
so polite and funny. You know when you meet someone

and you know you will be able to relax with them? He told me he was a designer and he was going to New York on business, I told him I worked on a fashion magazine, and I was going there on holiday. We found out we were staying at the same hotel, we liked the same music, we'd seen the same films, we agreed to meet for dinner, and... well... so on and so on, we don't have to go any further, because that is for me, and not for you. It changes a little every time I tell it, maybe he's in films and I'm an actress, but it is always very wonderful and exciting.

2001... that was a very good year for me.

*She takes the photo out of the diary. She looks at it.*

And sometimes, little one, I make up stories about you.

*Pause.*

Perhaps I go and see what has happened to that woman.

No, I wait here, like a good girl.

How old are you? It's a rude question, but I ask it anyway.

I'd say... *(say an age about a year older than they really are)*. It's hard to tell. Some of you look a lot older. Especially the girls. It's true, girls always look older than boys. We know how to make ourselves look eighteen, nineteen, twenty even. Boys can't do that. It's not fair, but that's the way it is. Another thing that's not fair – girls always want to go out with boys who are older than them. Yes? Maybe not all girls, some girls.

I had a boyfriend who was twenty-three when I was only fourteen. Not really a boyfriend, I was only sitting with him for two minutes, but he could have been if my father hadn't seen us. My father said, 'Are you friends with my daughter?' The boy says, very polite, 'I would like to be, but we have only just met'. My father says, 'Has she told you she's only fourteen?' I wanted to die, right that moment, or have a big flash of lightning strike my father down. I don't see that boy again ever, and I don't speak to my father for a month.

But truly, when he was saying about he was twenty-three, and I was very pretty, how he had such a nice car... you understand? I was a little scared. So I don't mind my father got rid of him, but I never tell him so.

*She picks up the picture of her sister.*

My sister. Thirteen years old when this was taken. Fifteen now.

*She looks at the objects on the desk.*

*She picks up the belt buckle.*

This belonged to my uncle, he was a very big man, I mean, very big, so he had to have a very big belt with a very big buckle. He used to wear his trousers up very high indeed, so all this bigness was behind his trousers, and not hanging out over the top. He liked to fish, and we would go with him. My sister liked my uncle very much. Because my uncle would say to my father not to be so strict with her, and my father would point to me and say 'look what happened with this one'. Which is another story.

One day, my sister wanted to swim in the river, my uncle said, no, she couldn't, then there was this big splash, and my sister was in the river, swimming across to the other bank. The current was very strong...

*Pause.*

But she was a very good swimmer and she got to the other side and was safe. The end.

When you see a story is going in the wrong way, stop it before it can go too far. A good story must learn to do what it's told.

*She goes to the door as if to open it. Stops.*

Where I grew up wasn't so different from here. / Where I grew up was very different from here. *(Select appropriate option.)*

A big block of flats, on the edge of a little town. We were on the bottom, so my mother let us play outside with the other children. There was a small playground. By the time I left, no mother would let her children out alone, and they had knocked down the playground and built a big wall that cut us off from everybody else, right across the street. I know why the council put it there, they must have found out that we had something horrible, that we could give to other people, like a plague. The wall was to keep everybody safe from us. I mean, nobody would build a wall to separate one from another without good reasons. So you are talking to an infectious person. What is this infection actually, I don't know, but until that woman fetches me to talk with your head teacher, I have to stay here, so I try not to breathe a lot in case you catch something.

Joke.

*Pause.*

We must find a good way to pass the time.

One of you must choose an object and I'll make up a story about it. Hey, don't look so worried. Do you think I am stupid? Put you in a horrible story? No thanks. I want to leave here in one piece.

No.

I came here to ask to speak to pupils, you are pupils, so I speak to you. Properly. Then if the woman who put me in here comes back and says 'No, you can't speak to them', you will say to others what I have said to you.

OK. I am in your country because I am a refugee. Asylum seeker. That's what you say. Well, I seek this asylum and I find it and I am now real British citizen. Very lucky girl.

But, of course, I don't have to tell you why I come here with my family, it is to take your jobs and your houses and not do any work and live for free on your generous benefits. It's true. It's what it says in your papers, it must be so.

It's such an easy thing to leave your country. Did you know that? One very beautiful, cloudless day you say to yourself, what shall I do? Some shopping? Help my grandmother? Go to the café and see my friends? Visit my cousins? Then you say, no, today, I shall do something different. I shall make a very long, very dangerous journey, leave my home, my friends, my family, and go and build a new home in a foreign country.

*Pause.*

What would it take to make you leave your country? I don't say for a holiday, for one or two years, but probably forever? Can you think of anything bad enough that might happen to you here to make you want to do that? No? Then you are very lucky people.

We left our home only after they built the wall across the street to keep us away from everyone else, only after they told me that I could no longer go to college to be a teacher, only after my mother was attacked and spat at, and my little brother had his leg broken by the boys he used to play with, but of course, it was an accident because they were such good boys and would never mean to do anything like that, and only after my cousin's house was burned to the ground, and they killed her husband, and stoned her and the baby she was carrying inside her. Those are good reasons to leave, I think.

*Pause.*

I tell you now why I am an infectious person, why they built a wall to keep us apart, then some of you will think, yes, I was right all the time about the rude nasty girl, please teacher come and send her away.

I'm Roma, a gypsy, a traveller. You know now what to expect, yes? I try to tell your fortune. Sell you some lucky charm. One of you should go and fetch a person to throw me out, you have a dirty gypsy in your class.

*Pause.*

I'm sorry.

That was rude of me. I should not say that I know what you will think.

Bad girl. Angry all the time.

*Pause.*

Calm now.

My father told my mother, my little brother, my sister and me we had to go. He said he would stay behind, someone had to look after the grandparents. But we told him, we go nowhere without you. The grandparents made him leave. They said that his duty was with us now. So how you think he feels? My cousin and her baby were in the hospital, and we wanted them to come with us too. Then, her baby died, and she said no, now she didn't care any more what happened to her, so she would stay with the grandparents. I tell you this so understand. This is not an easy thing that we have done.

Why we come here? OK. My mother's cousin has lived in Leeds since a very long time, she is a proper English person. We hoped we might go there, but we are grateful that they let us stay at all.

This is all complicated. And I start to have this anger again because I think I sound like I am saying sorry for being here.

If you are Roma, I don't want to say it is worse, you know, than if you are a black person, or Asian, or Chinese or anything else that people decide they want to hate, no, of course it isn't, but Roma, always we feel outside of everything and everybody. Some of our people say we should stay like that and we are only safe together. Everybody knows all about us, we are the children of the devil, we sell our daughters into marriage, we don't wash. Our children don't go to school, we steal, wherever we go we make everything dirty.

I am a clean girl, I promise you, I wash myself all the time, and my father, he wouldn't sell me, it would not be something he could think about.

If all your history is about you being kept outside everything all the time, for some it is not possible to change, to leave behind those things in your culture that are not the right things any more.

So, I don't tell you about the journey, you don't want to know anyway, it was horrible. But I tell you now we have a flat for all of us, not on the bottom this time but near the top. It is in Manchester, with a big view. My mother has a job cleaning in a hospital, my father works in a public park, as a gardener, he's very lucky, it's like the job he had at home. My brother is at school and does not want to know about anything but football. We send back what we can to the grandparents, and when my cousin writes us a letter she says things are not getting better, only worse.

We are trying to be a proper English family, like my mother's cousin.

I have been going to college, to improve my English, and for my exams – I do not give up, you see, teacher one day – but I have to pay for that with a stupid, what you call it, a Macjob? Horrible, but I can't study if I don't earn any money.

*Pause.*

I show you properly why I have come to your school.

*She holds up the picture of her sister.*

This is my sister. The one who jumped into the river? Look at it properly please.

My sister.

You have seen a face like hers, perhaps? I always hope that one day someone will say they have seen her? She has disappeared. That is why I am here. To ask if you know anything. No, listen, it is possible. Look.

*She takes an envelope out of her bag. She takes out a postcard. (The picture on the postcard should be of the place where the play is being performed.)*

It's not in English.

'I'm alright – please stop – don't try and find me.' She doesn't sign it. But it is from her.

She has sent me the card to say where she is, but she doesn't say anything more, I think perhaps because someone might see it and try to stop her. But I don't know.

It is not the first one. When I got the first one the police say she could be anywhere, not at the place on the postcard, but I say if I believe they are right and I am wrong I will have nowhere to go to look for her.

*She holds up her sister's picture.*

Remember this face, please. This is thirteen. Now she is fifteen. She won't look like this now, she will have changed, and we have spoken of how a girl can look when she wants to, but only just fifteen.

She worried my mother and father because they did not know the places that she was going to, where these places were, or anything about them. But it's normal. My sister got angry when they spoke to her, and said that they had to trust her, and that's normal too.

She met a boy, of course, she did. My brother started teasing her, that's how we found out. She wouldn't tell us anything about him. We didn't know if he went to her school, how old he was... My parents kept asking her, but the more they asked, the angrier she got. We talked about it, the three of us, we knew that she was in a different country, a different culture. We could not force her to do things. We said to each other 'it will pass', 'he's probably very nice', and 'she will let us meet him when she's ready'. We didn't believe any of the words we said, I'm not sure if I believed the boy was real until my father saw him.

*Pause.*

It was like it was with me. He saw her with this boy. In the street. Talking. He could tell straight away that this boy was not for my sister. Anyway, he was not a boy, he was a man.

*Pause.*

He went to talk to them. He asked the same question, 'Are you friends with my daughter?' but he didn't get the same reply. This one didn't even pretend to be polite. I won't tell you the words he said to my father, but you can guess. My father is a strong man, in every way, but he is not used to a young man speaking to him like this, and for a moment he doesn't know what to do.

He says to my sister to come away, and she says, I will come home later. He says, 'No, you will come home now, with me.' And it is then that he sees this man is not alone. Suddenly there are others, and they are all standing around my father. The man she is with tells him to go away, he doesn't say 'go away', he uses other words. To my father, in front of his daughter. Then they all start shouting that he should go home, back to his own country. That he is a 'bastard asylum', who thinks he can take their jobs and their houses.

They start to threaten him. They know where he lives, they will 'torch' his flat. They tell him that he needs a lesson from them. My sister can only stand there, because she is very frightened and she doesn't know what to do.

My father takes her arm to bring her home, and that is the moment that they hit him, from behind, across the back of his head with some kind of metal bar. He falls to the ground and they are beating him and kicking him until he loses his consciousness, and even afterwards too. I know because there are witnesses who spoke about this to the police. Which is their duty.

But I'd like to know why none of these witnesses could tell the police who did this to my father, and why none of these witnesses tried to help him?

When he had his consciousness again, there was a woman and a man from an ambulance looking after him, and my sister had gone.

These witnesses said she had gone with the men, but I know she was taken. She would never leave my father to lie bleeding in a street. She wouldn't. I know this for sure.

The police have her on their list as a missing person. They are looking for her. But she is not found. I went to her school and the head teacher, she let me talk to her friends about my sister. Some of them said that they knew she had a boyfriend, but none of them knew who he was, none of them knew anything about it at all. I didn't believe them, because they were frightened, and they were not frightened of me.

My father was so shocked. He had brought us to this country so that we would be safe. He kept saying, 'Why do they do this?'

I tell you what makes me most afraid – this man, the one who takes her – has not done this thing because he wants to be her boyfriend.

There is a part of Manchester called Fairfield Street. It can be a good place with bars and music and lots of students having a good time, I know because I have been there with some friends I made at my college. But it is also where a man goes when he wants to find a prostitute.

I go there. I talk to the women, some of them won't speak to me, some of them think that I am another foreign girl who will do it without a condom and make life bad for them, but some of them are very nice and helpful. But none of them can say they have seen my sister.

When I was there I saw some girls who were young like my sister. From all countries. Horrible.

I hope she is not on some Fairfield Street.

*Pause.*

After another six weeks, I get a postcard like the one I showed you, from Bolton. So I go there and speak to people. I get another one from Liverpool, one from Leeds, and I go to all these places and I talk to so many people, I go to all the bad parts of these cities, and I walk and walk until I have to go home again. I tell the police about these postcards, but I don't think they go and look for her anymore.

Last week I got the postcard that I have shown you.

Nearly two years it has been.

I don't want to think about all the things that have might have happened to my sister.

My family say I should think about my college and stop following postcards. That I should leave it all to the police.

*Pause.*

I don't expect a miracle, that you will find her for me. But I ask you to remember her face, the way it looks here.

*Pause.*

That is what I was going to ask your head teacher to let me talk about. But you have let me speak more from my heart than I could do in front of a lot of faces in a big hall.

*Pause.*

I think the woman who put me in here has forgotten about me, and when she remembers they will ask me to leave, because nobody knows who silly ranting girl can be, and we can't let foreign strangers talk to our pupils, so for me it is good that I have said it to you like this, and you have to listened.

That's it now. Nothing more to say.

Sometimes I think that maybe I stop. That my family are right. Don't interfere. Leave it to the police.

It's not everything I do. I study. I work. I have a boyfriend. I go to films. I laugh. Normal girl.

But she is my sister, and she is lost. I won't stop looking.

*Pause.*

The story with the buckle, by the river, when my uncle was fishing, and I didn't finish it? He jumped in and saved my sister, so that part of her story had a happy end. Maybe this time too. They can happen. Happy endings.

I don't think I wait any more. You can tell about my sister to your friends.

*She writes on the board.*

This is her name – Sofia.

*And this is my mobile.*

I leave you the number, if you think of anything, please ring me.

You have been very patient.

*She sorts out her things, puts her coat on, and puts her bag over her shoulder. As she turns to leave she puts her hand in her pocket and takes out some stones.*

These are from the river bank where my uncle fished.

*She selects a stone.*

I know there is a story in this one, but I can't find it.

*She turns to the student she asked to choose an object.*

You have it. I don't know, but I think maybe it will speak to you.

*Pause.*

Ciao.

*She leaves the room.*

*Lights down.*

*The end.*

# Production Images

## *A Girl With A Book*

*Nick Wood (writer and performer), at the New Nottingham Theatre*
*photo by Alex Esden*

*Right – from the 2004 performance of 'Traum weißer Pferde' at the*
*Theater Ingolstadt*

*A Dream of White Horses*

# Production Images

## *Mia*

*Ann-Birgit Höller, at the Dschungel Wein Theaterhaus (Vienna)*

# MORE PLAYS BY NICK WOOD

## *Warrior Square*
## Winner of The Brüder Grimm Prize, Berlin

The exciting story of two refugees, a brother and sister, and their escape from a war-torn country to England. Persecuted for being different, Andrea and Riva are forced to flee their homeland, and now they must learn to live in a country very different from their own.

'...shows us the extent to which children are capable of taking control of their own lives, and conquering the absurdities of bigotry and hatred...'
— Berlin Theatre Festival

£7.99  ISBN 0954691202  64 pages  Age range 8+

## *We Didn't Mean To Go To Sea* by Arthur Ransome *(adapted for the stage)*

Father is away and mother brings Roger, John, Susan and Titty to stay at Pin Mill where they can spend the summer messing about in boats. Their adventure begins when they go out with Jim on his boat *Goblin*. But disaster strikes when the boat is becalmed and Jim goes ashore to fetch petrol. Fog descends over the Harwich estuary and, as the tide turns, the boat begins to drift away ...

'There is a nice sense of period about these kids coping on their own under extraordinary, but quite believable circumstances, lisle pullovers and plimsolls at the ready but the human anguish between them is universal and timeless, although there are lots of laughs on the way, too. Highly recommended.'
— The Stage

£9.99  ISBN 9781906582050  96 pages  For family audiences

# Aurora Metro Books

## SOME OF OUR OTHER PLAY COLLECTIONS

**PLAYS FOR YOUTH THEATRES AND LARGE CASTS** by Neil Duffield

ISBN 978-1-906582-06-7 £12.99

**THEATRE CENTRE: Plays for Young People** introduced by Rosamunde Hutt

ISBN 978-0-954233-05-1 £12.99

**BLACK AND ASIAN PLAYS ANTHOLOGY** introduced by Afia Nkrumah

ISBN 978-0-953675-74-6 £12.99

**YOUNG BLOOD plays for young performers** ed. Sally Goldsworthy

ISBN 978-0-9515877-6-8 £12.99

**PLAYS FOR YOUNG PEOPLE** by Charles Way

ISBN 978-0-953675-71-5 £9.95

**THE CLASSIC FAIRYTALES Retold for the Stage** by Charles Way

ISBN 978-0-954233-00-6 £11.50

**THE CLASSIC FAIRY TALES 2 Retold for the Stage** by Charles Way

ISBN 978-0-955156-67-0 £11.99

**NEW PLAYS FOR YOUNG PEOPLE** by Charles Way

ISBN 978-1-906582-51-7 £12.99

**NEW SOUTH AFRICAN PLAYS** ed. Charles J. Fourie

ISBN 978-0-954233-01-3 £11.99

**BALKAN PLOTS: New Plays from Central and Eastern Europe** ed. Cheryl Robson

ISBN 978-0-953675-73-9 £9.95

**www.aurorametro.com**